Loving a "Difficult" Man

Loving a "Difficult" Man

*Affirmations for
Living, Learning,
and Loving*

Nancy Good

Adams Media Corporation
Avon, Massachusetts

Published by
Adams Media Corporation
57 Littlefield Street, Avon, MA 02322 U.S.A.
www.adamsmedia.com

ISBN: 1-58062-579-7

Printed in Canada

J I H G F E D C B A

Good, Nancy.
    Loving a "difficult" man : affirmations for living,
learning, and loving / by Nancy Good.
        p. cm
    ISBN 1-58062-579-7
    1. Man-woman relationships. 2. Men—Psychology.
I. Title
HQ801 .G59155 2001
306.7—dc21   2001046301

This publication is designed to provide accurate and
authoritative information with regard to the subject matter
covered. It is sold with the understanding that the publisher
is not engaged in rendering legal, accounting, or other
professional advice. If legal advice or other expert assistance
is required, the services of a competent professional person
should be sought.
        —From a *Declaration of Principles* jointly adopted by
            a Committee of the American Bar Association and
                a Committee of Publishers and Associations

Cover illustration by Capstone Studios, Inc.

*This book is available at quantity discounts for bulk purchases.
For information, call 1-800-872-5627.*

Visit our home page: *www.adamsmedia.com*

For Bruce—my wonderful brother
who knew how to love and live.

Contents

Acknowledgments

I want to thank my husband, Wendell Craig, and my daughter, Joanna, for their help on the manuscript and for their patience and self-reliance during the many hours I wrote behind closed doors. Thanks go to Joanne Goodspeed, Debra Hertz, Aimee Levy, Maureen Murray, Lena Furgeri, and the gang at the health club for their continuing support and friendship. Jennifer Lantagne and my editors at Adams Media have been invaluably helpful with editorial suggestions throughout the publication process. And, as always, thanks to my agent, Agnes Birnbaum, whose perseverance is truly astounding.

Introduction

Loving a difficult man presents a tiring and frustrating challenge to every woman. This book is intended to help you meet these challenges as you try to figure out how to have a good life with your current mate or as you look for Mr. Right and find that every man has a set of problems. Think of this as multi-vitamins for your inner loving self—practical help and support that will inspire and refuel you when you get run down from it all, along with pep talks to keep you aware of how special and unique you really are.

Each page begins with an affirmation and ends with an inspirational quote. Through these affirmations, stories and advice, you will learn how to be psychologically smarter about love and get a better understanding of how the unconscious mind and family background causes a man to act badly. Here you will also find the confidence to ask for and obtain "positive stroking"—the admiration, appreciation, and understanding you deserve, as well as advice about how to get a man to make a commitment and stay with it.

Your life may be so busy already, you don't have time to read another book. That's why each affirmation is short—providing a quick burst of support you can turn to in a free minute. Each page is like a good friend who offers the perfect words of encouragement when you've had a bad day, when you've lost faith in love and in yourself, and don't know what to do next. You'll find some advice, and just as important, you'll find a new way to believe in yourself.

You deserve to be happy, whether you are involved with a difficult man or are not in a relationship at all. These affirmations will bring you closer to that happiness. Here are tools to make you strong enough to deal with a man when he's almost impossible to deal with, so you can be the best and happiest you can be, with or without him.

From my twenty-five years of experience as a therapist working with women, I know that you *can* become happier even if the man in your life, or the one who could be waiting in the wings, is difficult. This simple but extremely potent idea can change your life.

Loving a "Difficult" Man can help you turn a bad day into a good one. One good day leads to another, and pretty soon you're having a string of good days; maybe even a week or two of good days; maybe finally a whole month. And presto—what a man does, or a friend or family member for that matter, will no longer affect you in the same way. You won't take it personally. You will have arrived at a very powerful time and place where you are in charge of how you feel— and no one can take that away from you.

This is called "detaching with love," a concept the 12-step programs have talked about for years. It is an essential concept to learn through practice, by trial and error—to separate yourself from the thoughtless or hurtful things a man might do.

Read these affirmations one day at a time or straight through to the end in a few days. It doesn't matter how quickly or how slowly you go. Reread the affirmations over time so that they stick to your psyche, and blend in with your personality. Some of the ideas will strike home for you more than others. Keep a list of those so you can turn to them when you're feeling troubled or need guidance.

It would not be fair to blame on men all the problems women have with them. Unconsciously, you are reliving some part of your childhood experience just as a man is reliving his. Thus here you will also learn how to become psychologically smarter about your own past too. As you get psychologically smarter and more confident, you'll gain the ability to break your own destructive patterns even if you've been with the same difficult man for years. Or you may choose to move on as you outgrow your old ways to find a different man who is easier for you to deal with.

ALL CHANGE TAKES TIME. That's worth repeating. Any changes, whether they concern your attitude or your man's, will take time. The mountains and seas did not arrive where they are overnight. Your psychological topography, and his, took time to develop. A new positioning of your psychological terrain can take years.

Life is truly a work of art in progress. And the process of creating and building your life will engage and intrigue you as much as achieving your goal. Have respect for your soul and your mind and your inner emotional life. Don't meddle with your head. People in your life have done that enough already. Let yourself be, but become self-aware.

Read these affirmations without any pressure at all that you or the man in your life must change. Rather, imagine them washing over you like a healing sea, allowing time for their meanings to sink in and enrich your emotional skin. You will be surprised to find that change will happen faster if you don't work at it. Just keep reading and relaxing, and change will happen at the right pace, at the right time, for you.

Part 1

Looking to the Past:
The Psychology of Love

~ 1 ~

*I like to think that romance is simple,
but I get hurt when men change from
hot to cold. I'm willing to understand
the psychology of romance.*

If you want to be powerful in a romantic
relationship, you've got to remember the
psychological term *transference*, which
means that each partner in a relationship
increasingly views the other as someone
from his or her past.

When Janet first met Peter, they
couldn't keep their hands off each other.
Peter, a project director for a contracting
firm, was enamored with Janet. For three
months they spent every night together.
At Peter's suggestion, Janet moved in. But
soon afterward, Peter began to complain of
feeling too tired at night for sex. What had
been passionate soon became perfunctory.

Janet was smart about transference.
She saw that Peter felt pushed around by

his mother and that he fought back by making promises to her he wouldn't keep. He wouldn't call his mother back for days. He'd promise to attend family functions and then wouldn't show up. Janet realized that Peter was reacting to what he perceived as her demands for sex the same way he reacted to his mother's demands. Janet stopped mentioning sex, and pulled away physically from Peter. She soon found that he no longer felt pressured, and their sex life resumed.

Now the real beginnings of the "freedom" . . . to finally discover all I had to do was reach inward, and it was there waiting all the time for me!
—*Alisa Wells*

~ 2 ~

*When a man has become emotionally
unavailable, I've blamed myself instead
of his psychological history. That's a
destructive thing to do to myself.*

Steve has been drifting in and out of
Sharon's life for two years. Sometimes
she doesn't hear from him for months
at a time. She's dated other guys, and
he's been with other women, yet he
comes back to her over and over again.
So far she hasn't met anyone who
makes her feel the way Steve does. But
he won't talk about commitment. The
worst part of this scenario is what
Sharon does to herself when Steve disappears. She spends weeks blaming herself in small and large ways for why he's
gone again. "If only I'd worn a sexier
outfit; maybe I had bad breath; I
shouldn't have had sex with him. Yes,
I should have had sex with him.

I shouldn't have called him on his birthday. Or maybe I should have. . . ."

The reason why Steve runs from commitment actually has nothing to do with Sharon. Rather, his behavior is rooted in the fact that Steve's mother left his father for another man when Steve was only five. Steve and his father never recovered. Deep down, Steve is terrified to pledge himself to one woman. In fact, Sharon should be flattered (in a weird way) that Steve is emotionally able to see her as much as he does. If Sharon wants commitment, she will have to move on and be willing to tell Steve that when he calls. If he gets scared enough, maybe he'll go for help. But she shouldn't plan her life around that possibility.

*The family—that dear octopus
from whose tentacles we never
quite escape . . .
—Dodie Smith*

~ 3 ~

*Although a man may try to blame
me because he isn't nurturing, I will
not accept responsibility for his
emotional stinginess.*

How will an emotionally stingy man
blame you when you ask him to nurture
you verbally? Here are some of the
destructive responses you could get
from him.

You say, "I love you," and ask him
to say the same to you, or you ask for a
compliment. He replies:

"What's the matter with you? Don't
you know how I feel?"

"You're trying to control me. Don't
tell me how to talk."

"Why should I tell you that you look
nice if you don't? Should I lie?"

"You're really needy, do you know
that?" or "You're too needy for me.
I need someone stronger."

"Why do you have to spoil every-thing when things are so nice?" Or the worst, "Who said anything about love? We just have a good time together."

He's insecure, feels controlled, feels incredibly needy himself and embarrassed about his needs, yet he wants to make sure no one finds out about it. He wants to be in a "one-up" position—being sure of your feelings and keeping you in the dark about his. Don't buy these excuses. It's not you who has the problem.

A stranger loses half his charm the day he is no longer a stranger.
—Geneviève Antoine Dariaux

I don't have to prove I'm right in a silly argument. Instead, I can understand that the reason this man has to argue is rooted in his past.

When your man's emotions or reactions seem to make no sense, this is a sign that a problem from childhood is rearing its ugly head. Use your psychological awareness, as Theresa did.

"I've been married to Carlos for two years. In the past year we've been having a problem. Each morning after we make love, Carlos is irritable and picks a fight with me. Last time it was about doing the laundry. The time before, it was about putting the cap back on the toothpaste. He just gets in this crazy bad mood and needs to fight.

"I remembered that Carlos once told me that as a child he'd hear his parents make love and then fight. His father might end up hitting his mother and storming out. He could hear his mother cry. When he makes love to me, I think he remembers those scenes. I think it makes him feel awful and that he picks a fight with me so he doesn't have to feel so sad. I'm just going to ignore him when he gets like this. It blows over. Maybe sometime when we're relaxed I'll explain what I see is going on."

Theresa didn't interpret Carlos's anger as being her fault. She understood his past and protected herself with that knowledge.

One of the few things human beings have to offer is the richness of unconscious and conscious emotional responses to being alive . . .
—Ntozake Shange

~ 5 ~

*When I look around at this man's
family, I can see why he isn't
nurturing. I may see the same problem
in my own family. It's not my fault
he is the way he is.*

Sometimes it's really clear how a man's
family sets up a lifetime of deprivation.
Sometimes it isn't. Ted's family looked
like a loving, generous family to Talia,
especially compared to hers. When Ted
and Talia got married, his parents paid
for living room furniture and a good part
of the honeymoon. They were pleasant
enough to her, but Ted was turning out
to be not so sweet once they were married. He seemed disinterested in most of
what Talia had to say, and he was cheap.
Despite their good combined incomes, he
never wanted to spend money on a real
vacation or go to a play or concert. Talia
snooped around and found that when

Ted was growing up, his father had hated vacations and used to take the family to awful campgrounds at best. Mostly they stayed home. His mother had gone alone to most music or theater events—her husband said they were boring. Ted's behavior reflected that of his parents, who hadn't enjoyed many good times together and who had told him to "stop whining" whenever he had tried to talk about problems.

If your man is depriving you, there must be a reason in his past. Look harder. It's not your fault.

Don't accept rides from strange men, and remember that all men are strange as hell.
—Robin Morgan

~ 6 ~

*His family doesn't want him to be a
man with feelings. His father was not
a model of how to communicate. I can
understand how hard it is for him to
be emotionally honest.*

Since you're on the receiving end of your
man's emotional iciness, it's really hard
to be sympathetic. Yet, he is suffering,
too, behind that wall he puts up.

Imagine the childhood experienced
by Evan, now a 35-year-old carpenter. His
father worked long hours as a construc-
tion worker and was irritable and impatient when he came home. When Evan
was four and whined about taking a bath
or going to bed, as most children do, his
father would curse at him, chasing him
into the bathroom or bedroom. If Evan
then cried out of fear, his father screamed
louder and would try to hit him if his
mother didn't intervene. As a result of

this treatment, Evan stopped whining and stopped crying, keeping an impassive mask to the world from the time he was five. As a child he hadn't even felt safe to show much happiness. His father hadn't liked laughter unless he was the one laughing first. Evan survived this childhood to become an emotionally withdrawn adult, closed off from his girlfriend.

The tragedy for so many men is that if they could let down their guard, they would have a far richer life than they have and be closer to their women. If your man is walled off but you can still feel compassion for him, you have a chance of slowly helping him overcome that background.

Happiness is no vague dream, of that I now feel certain. . . . One is happy as a result of one's efforts, once one knows the necessary ingredients of happiness.
—George Sand

~ 7 ~

*Today I will not criticize his family,
no matter what they've done,
and I will walk away when he
criticizes mine. I resolve to try
this more and more often.*

We all know that families can sometimes
be a pain but that we need them anyway.
And that while it's okay to complain
about your own family, we really don't
like others to put them down.

Anita is married to Jack. Jack's
brother was getting married and Jack was
the best man. Of course, Anita and her
parents were invited. Anita's sister lived
far away and happened to be planning a
visit that week. Anita asked if she could
be invited also. She never received an
answer. Finally, Jack's brother and his
fiancé decided there were too many
people coming already and Anita's sister
couldn't come. Anita was furious and

told Jack that his brother was a bastard and that his family was cheap and always had been. Jack, in turn, said he had never liked Anita's sister anyway. Anita and Jack came close to breaking up until Anita realized what a bad idea it was for them to battle over their families. The important thing was that they loved each other, even if they didn't love each other's families.

Don't hold each other responsible for the actions of family members.

I know that family life in America is a minefield, an economic trap for women, a study in disappointment for both sexes.
—Anne Roiphe

~ 8 ~

I won't come between a man and his mother (or his memory of her). I'll study his story and proceed carefully.

Whatever a man feels about his mother will have an impact on how he sees you. The only way to understand the impact is to study the situation. But don't jump to any conclusions. For example, it is not safe to assume that if a man's mother loves you, he will, too. For some men who dislike their mothers and try to do the opposite of what they want, your being loved by her could be the kiss of death to the relationship. On the other hand, some men who idealize their mothers will idealize you as well, which, of course, will work in your favor.

Men who have a negative history with their mothers about a specific situation, like finances for example, may be suspicious of you when it comes to that subject, but not about anything else. If a man's mother was a terrible cook whose dinners all came out of a can, he may be suspicious of your cooking and far more critical of it than it deserves. But it can also go the other way—anything you cook may seem great in comparison.

Seem confusing? The essential lesson to take away with you is that you need to study the relationship. When a man describes you in terms that seem to have nothing to do with who you really are, take out your microscope for a closer look at his life with his mother.

Prejudice not being founded on reason cannot be removed by argument.
—Samuel Johnson

~ 9 ~

When a man acts like a kid, I end up acting like his mother. That doesn't help me get the romantic life I want.

You just met this great-looking man at a party. He took your number. Amazingly, he called that Monday morning. You have a great conversation, and he says he'll call you back on Thursday to make plans for Friday night. He doesn't call Thursday night. You are annoyed. You think maybe you should have done something differently. Friday comes. It's three o'clock. The phone rings. It's him. He acts as if he's calling at the right time and day. You say, "Weren't you supposed to call on Thursday?" already sounding like his mom. He sounds apologetic, says that something came up at work and he couldn't get to a phone. You finally plan to meet after work at a restaurant at seven o'clock. You're there on time. You wait for an hour, then leave feeling furious and unattractive and ready to kill him. What you want to do is call him the next day and scream at him, "What an irresponsible bastard you are! You'll never amount to anything. Drop dead." Making this call, however, would end up making him feel wanted.

This is a prime example of a man who resents his mother for what he perceives as her harping at him, checking up on him, and engaging in endless power struggles with him. He is emotionally immature and, unconsciously, he gets every woman he meets to act like his mom. Don't let it happen to you.

Nothing consumes a man more
completely than the passion
of resentment.
—*Friedrich Nietzsche*

~ 10 ~

Today I will look over my family history to see what chapter I'm replaying with my man. I deserve a big pat on the back and no criticism. Self-awareness is hard to achieve.

Ariana says: "My man, Matt, is a flirt. He doesn't have sex with anyone else—it's all just talk. He also has women friends he goes out with if I'm busy. I hate this, but I married him. Now I feel jealous and sometimes accuse him of wanting to sleep with his good friend Rita. He blows up at me. I know Rita and that it's very unlikely he'd be romantic with her. But I go on and on anyway. I thought about that and remembered how my mother used to accuse my father of looking at other women too often. I would hear them arguing at night. And my father really was more attentive to other women than to me or my mom.

There's an old wound getting opened up for me with Matt and his group of women friends. Matt's not that bad, really. I have to deal with him and my feelings differently."

Ariana deserves a lot of credit for seeing the similarities between the past and the present. Now she can have more control over the way she deals with her feelings and Matt. She is not blaming herself. She looked at the past because she knew something was out of control inside her and she wanted a change.

I never found the companion that was so companionable as solitude.
—Henry David Thoreau

~ 11 ~

I have given men the status of
a "father." Men have distorted me
as well. When I'm with a man,
I'll keep alert for these distortions.

If he's just a man, why does he hold the
power of a father to scare or intimidate
or infuriate you? Why do you feel like
you need this man in order to survive,
when you're a perfectly capable
woman? Because of that psychological
process called *transference,* in which feelings, originally associated with your
family, become unconsciously trans-
ferred to others.

There is no couple on earth on
whom transference does not have an
impact, so don't be ashamed to own this
meditation as your own. Be proud that
you are a step ahead of the crowd, and
smarter than most. When you realize
that you've given him the status of your

parent or teacher, he instantly becomes less powerful.

Consider Nadine, who used to flirt with every man she encountered and always slept with them on the first date. She was distraught when men did not call again. After years of this, she sought help. She realized that her father's only interest in her had been sexual. He used to leer at her and make inappropriate comments when she was young. Other than that, he had never talked to her. Nadine had turned each man she met into her father, and had figured that they'd only see her as a sex object—and that otherwise she was worthless. Once she understood this, her relationships improved.

What dire offense from am'rous causes springs.
What mighty contests rise from trivial things.
                              —Alexander Pope

*I have to look at my own background
to understand why I always wait for
him to apologize first.*

Kathryn is a very successful TV producer
who has never been successful with men.
Now thirty-five, she is experiencing the
breakup of another relationship. She and
Bart had a fight that started over their
political differences and kept going. She
called him a male chauvinist pig, he called
her a ball-busting woman, and they
haven't spoken since. Kathryn knows
deep down that they were both at fault,
but she still insists that he apologize first.
She has found herself in this position
many times before, as she can become
very impassioned about her views.

Kathryn clings to "being right" as
being everything—which is the way she
survived growing up with a domineering
mother. She's afraid to acknowledge

when someone else has a point, because she fears that he will humiliate her. So Kathryn waits for the man to "give in" before she will be nice to him. This way she feels safe. But she is losing good men who may be stubborn but are far more flexible and loving than she imagines.

It is nice when a man apologizes first. But you lose nothing and gain everything when you take the first step. If your man doesn't follow your lead and apologize after you do, then he may not be the flexible, honest guy you want.

It is only the first step that is difficult.
—Marie de Vichy-Chamrond

~ 13 ~

I don't want any man to have the
power to throw me into despair.
I'll take charge and look into my
history to see what else is adding
to the sadness.

Despair that intrudes on your thoughts
and depression that prevents you from
enjoying your day because your man has
done you wrong are not caused by your
man alone. The devastation in your gut
has its roots not with your romantic life
today, but in your past. There is some ele-
ment of loss and sadness that is the same
now as it was when you were a child.

Trish, a pianist and singer, says her
parents doted on her. Yet she feels terribly
depressed because Troy, her husband,
rarely goes to her piano performances.
Although others praise her, he does not,
and it ruins her achievement. She talked
about this with her brother, who

reminded her that their mother had done all the praising and that their father had stood by and nodded, but had never said anything. Trish realized that she had always wanted her father to praise her and tell her how he felt.

She decided to try to get her father, who was still living, to talk to her now. It was worth the effort, as she eventually got him to come to her performances and to open up to her. The depression lifted.

You have to sniff out joy;
keep your nose to the joy trail.
—*Buffy Sainte-Marie*

~ 14 ~

If a man is not interested in sex,
I don't need to run and get a makeover.
I should look at his family for clues
and find out what troubles him.

The hardest rejection to take is sexual. When you don't feel wanted sexually by your man, it's so easy to lay the blame on yourself. As women, we feel especially vulnerable about how attractive we are, anyway. Even runway models and beauty queens blame themselves when rejected in bed by a man they love. In this area of rejection, you have to be especially careful. First, relabel the sexual rebuff as your man's issue. After all, nothing has changed about you. If a person has real complaints in this area, it is that person's responsibility to share them with his or her partner.

Next, you'll need those psycholog-ical skills you've been honing. Observe your man's family carefully. Ask questions about his parents' marriage. Do you think they had a good sex life? Also be aware that health problems can easily affect a man's sexual functioning. If he's feeling inadequate or unsuccessful at his job, he's not going to be feeling very virile with you, either. These factors are far more crucial to your man's libido than whether or not you lost that extra five pounds.

*Though we travel the world over
to find the beautiful, we must carry
it with us or we find it not.*
—Ralph Waldo Emerson

~ 15 ~

*I have blamed myself when a man
runs away from commitment. But his
history is the culprit, not me. I realize
that the way other people behave
is their issue, not mine.*

Andrew is a real "commitment phobe,"
as Arlene calls him. He's warm with her
one minute, murmuring words of love
when they have sex, then disappears for
weeks at a time, only to reappear
swearing eternal love again. During the
four years she's known him, Arlene has
become psychologically smart about
Andrew. She knows that his father was
an alcoholic and hit his mother. She
understands that Andrew never knew
when his home would be calm or
chaotic. Arlene realizes he's afraid of
becoming an alcoholic himself and of
mistreating her if they lived together.
But Andrew hasn't put this together for

himself yet. He blames his absences on his reporting job.

Because Arlene knows so much she does not berate herself when Andrew disappears. She's through with lecturing him about his problems or trying to get him to go for help, because he refuses to do anything about it. Arlene realizes that she will have to stop seeing Andrew if she wants to find a man who will build a home and family with her. Andrew may suddenly decide he'll marry her if Arlene leaves him, but she cannot count on that.

How many really capable men are children more than once during the day?
—Napoleon Bonaparte

~ 16 ~

*Before I start pushing to get married,
I'd better learn to think
psychologically, not personally.*

Becoming psychologically smart is essential if you're the one who wants to get married and your man is hesitant or against the idea. If you don't understand his past, you'll walk straight into the wall of his anxiety and suspicion and wind up in turmoil.

Moira brought up marriage after she'd been living with Victor for a year. "I was shocked because Victor said, 'Marriage is for suckers. I didn't know that's what you had in mind. I'll pretend you never mentioned it.' I was very hurt, until my friend asked me why Victor had a problem with marriage. That got me thinking psychologically, not personally. Victor's father had left the house when he was five. His father had been a gambler and a good-time guy who never stayed with a woman very long. Realizing this, I became more sympathetic to Victor's issues with marriage. I could understand why he thought marriage never works and only causes trouble. I calmly asked him if he thought maybe his attitude had something to do with his parents. And he agreed. We're still talking about it, but we're not arguing like we were."

Think psychologically about yourself, as well. Did you pick your man with your eyes closed for some reason? Ask him how he feels about marriage before you move in together.

When a girl marries, she exchanges
the attentions of many men for
the inattention of one.
—Helen Rowland

*I'll locate the source of my patterns
in my past, so I can stop replaying
the same scenes with men over
and over. I can do this.*

You can blame a man for making your
life a shambles, but in the end, you'll
need to know why you didn't walk away
from the relationship. Except in a very
small number of situations, you are in
control of your life with any man.

Bridget's husband is possessive to
an extreme. When she goes out with a
friend, she has to call as soon as she gets
to the destination, and her husband
insists on always picking her up. Her
husband goes with her to buy clothes.
What he doesn't like, she doesn't buy.
She consults him on every decision, from
paint colors to what to eat for breakfast.
When she made plans to take a course
without asking him, he flew into a rage.

Bridget was terrified he would leave and dropped the course.

Bridget's husband is acting out a role for Bridget. Bridget has chosen him to play domineering father with her, but she doesn't have to play the little girl anymore. There are many people and places ready to give her the support she'll need to transform herself into the adult woman she really is.

Examine the contents, not the bottle.
    —*The Talmud*

Part 2

Clearing the Path to Romance

~ 18 ~

I no longer seek men on white horses.
The rescuer lies within me.

Which of the following two women
would you rather be?

Laurie lives with Eddie. Eddie often
goes out with the guys after work and
will call home at the last minute. The
first few times this occurred Laura was
upset, but not devastated. She stayed
home and went to bed early. The fourth
time she called a friend; they saw a
movie and had dinner together. They
laughed about guys and how impossible
they are. Eddie was surprised that she
was still out when he came home. He's
been getting home earlier these days.

Then there's Paula, whose boyfriend
Rick doesn't like her friends. One night
they argued about going to a thirtieth
birthday party for a friend of hers, and
Rick stormed out of the house. Paula

cried and tensely waited for him to return. By the time he got home it was too late to go to the party. She didn't think of calling a friend to go to the party with or going by herself.

Who would you rather be? The answer is obvious. When the man in your life acts in ways that are not good for you, turn to others who will be there for you when you reach out. Never cut yourself off from your support network.

Any woman who lets a man walk over her is a dumb idiot and deserves no better.
—Edith Piaf

~ 19 ~

*Blood is thicker than water.
Criticizing his family gets me in
trouble every time. I resolve to keep
my thoughts to myself.*

One way to get around fighting about family is to use your sense of humor and both acknowledge that of course you're each going to vote for your own family in the "who has the best" contest. Don't try to convince each other to love your family. He doesn't have the same history and ties to your sister that you do, for example, so don't push it. You should, however, ask for, and expect, politeness from each other when it comes to spending time with family.

We all have a knee-jerk reaction when it comes to our families. Joe, for instance, admits that his mother, an alcoholic, is impossible. As a child, he had to take care of his siblings when she was drunk. She could be nasty. But if *Nancy* complains about how awful Joe's mother is when she's drunk, Joe gets furious and might even counterattack with something about Nancy's mother, whom he in fact really loves and treats as his own mother.

We are all connected to our families. If a member of the family is criticized by an outsider, the family rises to the defense. When you both acknowledge that you have this family feeling in common, you'll find it easier to treat each other's family respectfully and resolve issues reasonably.

Never answer a critic, unless he's right.
—Bernard M. Baruch

~ 20 ~

Family bashing is destructive.
I won't speak against his family;
he can't speak against mine.

There are few rules that hold true for
every man and woman in a relationship,
but this is one of them. Never criticize
his family, even if he criticizes them first.
And he shouldn't criticize yours. Just
remind him, "Don't say anything about
my family, please. You know you
wouldn't want me to criticize yours." He
might respond, "Be my guest. I can't
stand my mother, anyway." But you are
smarter than that. "No, this is bad for
our relationship."

No matter what, he'll defend his
family deep down. As will you. The
reason is that lodged in each of us are
what therapists call *introjects,* the voices
of our parents and other relatives from
the past. It takes years of self-awareness

to be able to sort out your unique voice from those of the introjects. If he makes a comment about your mother, it will feel as if you've been badly insulted. This is a universal sensation. Become psychologically smart about how his family affects who he is today. But don't talk about your insights in a critical way to him. Only once in awhile and with compassion.

Love consists in this, that two
solitudes protect and touch
and greet each other.
—Rainer Maria Rilke

21

*I'm just as good as these cool, aloof
men. I refuse to be intimidated
by the masks they wear.*

Aloof, emotionally distant men may
intimidate you with their "in-control,
nothing-can-touch-me" attitude. But keep
in mind that underneath that attitude a
man is insecure and has a need for emotional connection. He is certainly not
better than you, nor emotionally
stronger. If you want to be like Orphan
Annie, having it as your mission to bring
to life an emotionally limited man, make
sure he has as much to give back to you
as Daddy Warbucks. Only give to men
who will appreciate you and give to you
in return. Remember not to misinterpret
a man's cool distance as a sign that he is
stronger than you are.

When a cool, in-control guy
becomes ill, you see the veneer crumble.

When Mayor Giuliani of New York was diagnosed with cancer, for example, he suddenly became "human," according to popular opinion. In-control men can choose to be "human" any time they want—and when the crisis is past, they can choose to be "cool" again. Defenses are very stubborn, and the wall can quickly be built back up. Don't mistake a man for a charity project. He will only change if he wants to.

Only about 10 percent of [a man]
is his intellect—the other
90 [are] his emotions.
—Dr. Mabel Ulrich

22

*Just because a man wants to keep
his distance emotionally doesn't
make him a healthier or stronger
person than I am.*

The guy who says, "I need a lot of
space," and is out of relationships faster
than a rabbit, is scared of something—yet
the movies make this man into a strong
type. He is shown kissing his woman
tenderly before he walks out the door.
He's off to climb a mountain, or join the
cavalry, or go to sea. The woman cries
and is bereft without him. She swears
loyalty till he returns. But wait a minute;
he's not all that brave—he wants to go.
He's more scared at the thought of
staying and dealing with the emotional
issues in a relationship.

Bill says he needs "space." Patty has
been with Bill for years and has suffered
because Bill regulates their togetherness

like he's adding salt and pepper to a stew. They move in together, a few months go by, and Bill decides he wants to live alone again. Whenever Patty wants to take a vacation with Bill, he decides to go off with his buddies. Patty feels rejected after each of these experiences. She relives bad memories of waiting for her father to visit her after her parents divorced. Patty is working hard at this meditation and at realizing that Bill is not healthier than she is because he wants distance—he's just playing out an old power struggle with her.

Women have changed in their relationship to men, but men stand pat just where Adam did when it comes to dealing with women.
—Dorothea Dix

~ 23 ~

My anxiety about emotional distance is understandable, but I don't have to let anxiety control how I act with a man.

Most women are more comfortable with a close romantic relationship than with a distant one because for centuries women were the keepers of the hearth. Although that is not often the case today, your anxiety may still get in the way of finding a comfortable distance in a relationship. Look at his desire for regular nights out with the guys as an opportunity for you to see your own friends and build your own interests instead of seeing it as a rejection, which it is not. If you're the kind of woman who obsesses when a man doesn't call, it would be a good idea to get some counseling to give you confidence and inner serenity.

Maybe you're a woman who needs a lot of space. Sarah, for example, lived with Fred for a year, and began to feel impatient and annoyed around him. She realized she needed some time away with friends and went to a spa for a weekend. When she came back she felt more loving toward Fred. Sarah scheduled regular weekends with friends after that. Fred was upset about being left alone at first—just like a woman might be! But he soon decided to go fishing with the guys those weekends Sarah was away. Their time together improved dramatically.

Constant togetherness is fine,
but only for Siamese twins.
—Victoria Billings

~ 24 ~

It's tough to remember on a daily basis,
but I'll give, and work on getting from
a man, the nurturing comments that
will hold us through the bad times.

Here's Dana's story: "Last year was the
worst of my life. A new boss came in and
fired a bunch of us to put in his own
people. Then my father got very ill and
almost died. In the midst of this I was
trying to get pregnant. Finally I did, but I
was driving with a friend and there was an
accident. I miscarried. My husband, Jack,
is not always the most understanding guy.
He was concerned and with me through
the first two crises, but when I lost the
baby he was more upset about his loss
than about mine. I felt he blamed me. We
were near to breaking up. He can be so
warm and loving to me when he wants to
be—like a cheerleader on my team when
someone treats me badly. That's what I

thought about when he became cold and distant after the miscarriage. I remembered how great he can be."

Jack had a good enough track record of being supportive and loving, so that when the miscarriage occurred and he directed his anger and disappointment at Dana, their relationship was able to survive. At some point in a long-term relationship, a couple may have to deal with a major crisis such as the death of a loved one, a serious illness, financial difficulties, a layoff, or problems with children. The foundation you have laid with your partner will help your relationship to weather these storms. The nurturing comments, loving endearments, and expressions of admiration and commitment you share with each other will act as the mortar that holds the foundation together.

How do I love thee? Let me count the ways.
—Elizabeth Barrett Browning

~ 25 ~

Any time I've used phony flattery to get a man, the relationship hasn't lasted for long. Praise needs to come from a sincere place, not out of manipulation.

Even Scarlett O'Hara, a master of manipulation, lost out in *Gone with the Wind*. She faked love and falsely flattered Rhett Butler for so long that he no longer believed her to be sincere by the time she had really grown to love him. His distrust was larger than his love. It used to be that a woman had to depend on a man to support her, so it made good business sense to flatter him insincerely and to study his interests to the exclusion of her own—to basically become an appendage of him. A relationship was a business deal, not necessarily a love match. But your options are wide open now. You don't have to wipe yourself out to survive with a man.

Give him compliments and thank him when you really mean it in some way. Often you must put your anger aside, change your tone, and act more understanding than you feel in order to heal a bad situation. You will lose yourself, and your man, if you are really lying when you say you think he's great. So say it when you mean it.

This is what I know:
Lovers' oaths are thin as rain;
Love's a harbinger of pain—
Would it were not so!
—Dorothy Parker

~ 26 ~

*It's actually fun when a man and
I are confident enough to admit to
each other that we feel jealous.
Then we both feel desirable.*

Jodie and Roger are an ideal couple. They
are secure enough to express their insecurity, and neither of them puts the other
down when he or she shares feelings.
Jealousy is allowed, even enjoyed. This
was the conversation they had as they
dressed to go to a barbecue at their
friends Toby and Bob's house.

"You're looking especially good,"
comments Roger. "Are you wearing that
for Bob? I notice how he looks at you
sometimes." Jodie responds, laughing,
"As if he doesn't look at everyone that
way. I do love it when you're jealous."
She kisses him on the cheek. "What
about when you wiped the barbecue
sauce off Sandra's [another friend]

blouse? She loved every swipe, believe me." Roger beams and they hug, reassuring each other that they are always loyal to each other and proud that their partner is attractive to others.

Roger and Jodie as individuals and as a couple are secure enough to allow for jealousy and to reassure each other so that each of them feels more desirable. When flirtations are hostile, covert, and consciously or unconsciously designed to make the other person crazy with jealousy, it's an indication that serious, insecure feelings are the cause and help is needed.

One must not lose desires.
They are mighty stimulants to
creativeness, to love, and to long life.
—Alexander A. Bogomoletz

*Since men have serious issues with
control, it's amazing that a man
can do what I ask. He deserves
appreciation even for small things.*

By the time he does what you asked him
to do, you don't praise him for it because
you think, "Well, what was the big deal?
He should have done this to begin with."
Maybe that's true, but you're forgetting
that he came to you already feeling controlled. Sure, there are some men who
are very cooperative about day-to-day
things, but watch out! They have a different set of problems.

Carrie wanted Phillip to watch the
kids on Saturday so she could take a
course. After weeks of negotiating, he
agreed. When the day came, he ended up
sitting around the house with the kids.
They snacked all day while he watched
TV—he even forgot to give them lunch.

The following week, Carrie made plans for Phillip to take the kids to a museum and to the park. Phillip carried out the plan, but Carrie never thought of praising him. So many of us are used to giving only negative feedback—we pay more attention to people who act badly or who say hurtful things to us than to people who are good to us. A man may think, what's the payoff for being nice? Why should Phillip make an effort to be cooperative when Carrie pays more attention to him when he's difficult? It takes a real effort, but it is important to build enthusiastic praise into your relationship.

*I can see that the Lady has a
genius for ruling, whilst I have
a genius for not being ruled.*
—Thomas Carlyle

~ 28 ~

A man's point of view can sound really crazy to me. I'll try to understand what he says even though it doesn't make sense from where I stand.

How can you understand his point of view when it just sounds nuts? It is possible, though it takes work. Joanne's fiancé John, for instance, thinks getting together with friends is a waste of time. He doesn't enjoy people or want to see anyone socially other than family members. Joanne thinks he's crazy. She's tried it his way, but not seeing friends gets pretty old real fast. Although they've agreed that Joanne should be able to see friends whenever she wants to, she feels like a third wheel with the couples she knows. Yet she doesn't want to break up over this. Joanne has tried both reasoning and arguing with

John, but hasn't been able to change his mind.

Once Joanne accepts that John has a right to his point of view, she'll be able to see that because John interacts with lots of people all day at a high-pressure job, he wants to withdraw on weekends and after work. He's also in a power struggle with Joanne, as he was with his mother who was socially prominent and showed him off to company. If Joanne understands John's reasons for being reclusive, she will not be as angry. She can also feel flattered that she's the only one he likes to be with. This should decrease the tension so they can enjoy being together again.

A man convinced against his will
is not convinced.
—*Laurence J. Peter*

*I can learn to read a man's emotional
sign language. Then I won't be in
the dark about his behavior.*

George drives Marnie crazy, but to
everyone else he's Mr. Nice Guy. He's
always willing to pitch in to help a friend.
But if Marnie asks him to fix a broken
lawnmower, for example, a friend's car
will come first. One weekend he said he
would help Marnie paint, but then told
her he had left something at the office
and stayed away all day. Marnie screamed
at him until she lost her voice, while he
just stood there looking hurt. All he had
done was to spend time talking with his
boss and then helping a motorist whose
tire was flat, he said. George is always
sweet and always has a reason why he's
been unavailable to Marnie. He has no
awareness of his inner feelings, but they
are revealed by his actions.

George's actions say to Marnie, "I feel controlled and like a little kid, and I don't want to do anything you ask. I'm a very angry guy in sheep's clothing." The anger started, of course, when he was a child. Marnie doesn't have to let him drive her crazy. It would be better for her if she kept her anger to herself and thereby deprived him of the motivation for his bad behavior. At some point she could suggest that perhaps he feels controlled. She could say she understands not liking to feel pressured to do what people ask of you. But first, she has to learn to read his emotional sign language.

Love doesn't just sit there, like a stone; it has to be made, like bread, re-made all the time, made new.
—Ursula K. LeGuin

~ 30 ~

*The cool attitude that a man
can have intimidates me, but
I know his emotional needs are
the same as mine. I won't lose
myself because of the coolness.*

You know the message men have
received since birth: Don't act as if you
care; don't act as if you need anyone very
much. When it's cold, don't admit you're
freezing; when you hurt yourself, ignore
the pain. Men have also been trained to
ignore emotional pain. Maybe you've
seen a man cry at a funeral, but that's
probably the only time. So it may be hard
to believe your man has the same emotional needs you do when he always
shows up late, doesn't call, or is annoyed
when you're sick or when you need his
attention. Just wait until *he* has the flu, if
you want to see how needy he really is.
Mr. Tough Guy needs you, believe me.

You've got to believe in your man's vulnerability if you're going to take a stand with him. Don't be intimidated and fooled by his cool attitude. As soon as he feels the connection with you weaken, he'll be responsive. Don't make the mistake of backing down from what is important to you because of his smirk or sneer. He's not as tough as you are. Statistics show that women are better at surviving alone than men are.

Men need women more
than women need men;
and so, aware of this fact,
man has sought to keep woman
dependent upon him.
—Elizabeth Gould Davis

~ 31 ~

*Even if a man acts as if he's
John Wayne, feelings scare him
more than I can tell.*

Here's an example of a man acting in an especially unfeeling way. It was the day of Becky's father's funeral. She and her boyfriend Bob were getting ready to leave for the chapel. Becky started to sob. Bob said in an angry voice, "Why don't you get a hold of yourself? You're not a baby." Becky was shocked and hurt, but she'd heard him talk like this before. She finished getting dressed in silence and felt more alone and devastated than ever.

You may find it impossible to try and be understanding of a man like Bob, but it will help Becky's self-confidence if she realizes that Bob is completely terrified of feelings like grief or sadness. That is why he is emotionally unable to hold her while she cries and why he called her a baby. When a man has a strong negative reaction to your feelings, he is scared. His reaction has nothing to do with you. If Becky truly believes this, she can later ask Bob what funerals were like for him—who cried, what happened. She might hear an earful. She can also quietly tell him what she needs from him in the future and add that she knows it's hard for him to act in the gentle way that she needs but she knows he can do it.

It's the most unhappy people
who most fear change.
—Mignon McLaughlin

~ 32 ~

I'll try to let go of blame.
Men just get more rigid when
they're told they're at fault.

Renee has been married to Alan for eight
years. Alan has a hot temper and flies off
the handle at small things, like their son
spilling a glass of milk at dinner. He gets
furious if they have to sit in traffic and
criticizes such things as Renee's driving,
the way she disciplines their son, and
her cooking. Her way of dealing with
Alan's temper is to yell back at him.
Renee calls him names, tells him he's
ruining their family, blames him for
every unhappy moment they've ever had.
Sometimes she brings up his mother,
whose hot temper is legendary, and she
blames everything on her. After eight
years of yelling back at him, nothing has
changed. Alan is more set in his rages
than ever. By now he thinks Renee is a

shrew and he takes no responsibility for his own problems.

Attaching blame to Alan makes Renee feel temporarily better but actually makes things worse—for her son, who can't stand the yelling. Afterwards she also feels bad about the way she's acted. It's time for her to stop blaming Alan and to stop yelling, no matter what he does. Renee must walk away when he starts in so that he will be left alone with the silence after he yells. That way, he might be able to hear how awful he sounds. Later, she can ask him, "How do you think it makes our son feel when you yell and criticize? Do you want your child growing up in this kind of atmosphere?"

I change myself, I change the world.
    —Gloria Anzaldua

~ 33 ~

I have a generous spirit and will
work on sharing it with a man,
even though at times my anger
is stronger than my generosity.

You can always find something nice to say to a man. If he changes a light bulb, watches the children, wears a new shirt, or acts politely around your sister whom he can't stand, tell him how much you appreciate him and how terrific, nice, and generous he is. Tell him you love him when you're feeling it for no reason at all. When your man does something you have asked for, even battled him for, it is imperative that you thank him and praise him.

Josie argued for weeks with Dick about going to Canada. She was furious that he wouldn't do this for her. She made her own plans and he finally said he'd go, but Josie was too angry to be nice. "He should have said yes at the beginning. Now he's spoiled everything," she said. The trip was tense and not fun for either of them. Josie had a pattern of twisting Dick's arm to get him to do what she wanted and then not thanking him. So each time she asked him to do something he would become more resistant. From Dick's point of view, he received more attention by saying no than by saying yes. How different it could be if Josie praised him lavishly whenever he did what she wanted. If she learned to let go of the grudge, Dick would feel appreciated and loved. The air would clear and love would emerge.

Come live with me, and be my love,
And we will all the pleasures prove . . .
        —*Christopher Marlowe*

*I won't freeze when a man is being
self-destructive. I can stay out of
his web of destruction.*

Marla is a smart, streetwise woman who
grew up in a Detroit working-class neigh-
borhood and rose above her roots; now
she's a vice president at a pharmaceutical
company. She has lived with Dave for five
years and makes more money than he
does. They each pay half the expenses.
Since Dave has never been happy as a
lawyer for a bank, he looks for business
excitement outside of his job. Once Dave
got Marla to give him money toward the
invention of a new kind of hammer. She
lost it all.

Dave's new idea is to open a skating
rink. Marla pointed out the reasons why
she didn't think this would make money.
She told him he would be nuts to spend
every penny he has and borrow against

his retirement account. But he went ahead and decided to take a loan to put more cash into the deal. Marla said that if his venture went bankrupt she would leave him, because she didn't want to support him. This last threat got through. Dave invested what he had but didn't take out a loan. He did lose everything. But at least Marla was able to stop him from even worse destruction and protected both herself and their relationship.

Man is a broken creature, yes . . . but it is also his nature to create relationships that can span the brokenness.
That is his first responsibility.
—Lillian Smith

~ 35 ~

*I'll try not to use work to
avoid intimacy, even if he's
using work to avoid me.*

If you're a workaholic, you may use
work to avoid feelings. Maybe you're
irrationally afraid of financial ruin, or
anxious about being "worthless." Or you
may feel that unless you're producing, no
one will love you and that if you work
hard enough, you will get the love and
attention you crave. Women with children who also have jobs are workaholics
because they have to be. This is not
about them.

   Linda worried that her husband
Craig didn't want to spend time with her,
that his job was more interesting to him
than she was. Linda knew that Craig's
job was demanding, but it seemed that
the people he worked with were able to
work less. When Linda met Craig he'd

had the same job and had been able to go out in the evenings. Now that they were married, she rarely saw him.

Never blame yourself when your man is working all hours. He may have issues about being close to a woman and feeling controlled. He may fear his boss for irrational reasons or be afraid his coworkers might think he doesn't put in enough hours—or he may have a pressing need to be successful to avoid depression. If you see his workaholism as his problem, not yours, you may be able to help him put work into perspective. And always keep your own life going.

If people are highly successful in their professions they lose their senses. . . . They lose their sense of proportion— the relations between one thing and another.
—Virginia Woolf

~ 36 ~

Bad habits like name-calling and faultfinding disappear slowly. I'll stay strong and calm while I work on this.

To be centered and goal directed in the middle of the storm is what will ultimately get you what you want, whether it is from your man, your work, your friends, or your life.

Susan met Doug through a personal ad. He was ten years older and definitely set in his ways. Susan could take his fussiness in cooking and that her things had to occupy one particular shelf in the bathroom when she slept over. But Doug had a bad habit of cursing intensely under his breath any time he was frustrated—if a glass broke, if the computer had a glitch, if another driver cut him off. The cursing made Susan tense. One day Doug even cursed at her during an argument about a political issue. When Doug wasn't spouting four-letter words, he was a nice man whom Susan enjoyed. But she could see that disagreements sparked a bad part of him. When she tied to talk to him about this they had a fight, and she ended up calling him a bastard and ridiculing his "stupid, prissy habits."

Patterns that emerge during arguments were created in childhood and take time to change. Since Susan wants to stay with Doug, she must think to herself, "This is his problem. I'll stay away from him till he calms down. I will try to breathe deeply and relax." Susan will also see if Doug will go with her to couples therapy.

Be not afraid of growing slowly,
Be afraid only of standing still.
—Chinese proverb

~ 37 ~

Old habits are hard to break, but let today be the day that I walk away when a man is verbally abusive. This will deprive him of his ability to hurt me emotionally.

Sometimes what may seem like an impossible situation may only require a change on your part to make it better. But making the change can be very hard to do. Walking away from a man who verbally attacks you can be a difficult pattern to break if you were used to being treated this way as a child. You might feel frozen in place and powerless when the attacker starts in with "You did this," or "You never . . ." or "The trouble with you is . . .". You must, however, walk away from outbursts that harm you emotionally. You can try saying, "Don't talk to me like that," but that is usually like pouring a pint of water on a forest fire.

It won't stop a verbally abusive man. Don't start defending yourself or explaining yourself to him, and don't stand there and take it. An out-of-control person cannot be reasoned with. Leave the room—and the house if necessary. Say you'll be back later. There is nothing you've done to make you deserve such an outburst. Wait him out. Don't try to make nice unless he is being nice first. Stand your ground while you wait for a decent level of communication from him.

People who cannot feel
punish those who do.
—May Sarton

38

*I've got enough of my own emotional
baggage. I don't want to carry a
man's emotions for him.*

You are a courageous woman who has
experienced many different feelings and
you have survived the emotional battle.
Most men, however, have little experience being aware of their feelings—for
some, it's as if their mental muscles are
not geared up for emotional exercise. So
you, with your stronger mental muscles,
may tend to act as the conduit for the
range of feelings you both experience.

Let's say you've had a relaxing day,
but your man has not. You meet him and
suddenly feel anxious and fearful. You're
feeling his feelings for him and are experiencing what therapists call "induced"
feelings. Ask a few questions, and you'll
hear about a work problem, a family
problem, a fight with another driver.

But be careful not to get filled up with feelings that are not your own—this can happen in any situation when you are unaware ahead of time that the person you are with has had a bad time. Don't accept emotional hand-me-downs.

The past is but the beginning
of a beginning.
—H. G. Wells

39

I have put too much energy into
men who don't give back. I will only
invest my emotional energy with
a man who is worth it.

Every relationship takes work. Every man
can be difficult in some way. But if you
expend energy on every man you meet,
you'll be exhausted very quickly. Don't
do what Gloria did. She was set up on a
blind date by a coworker. The guy turned
out to be a real loser, as even Gloria
described him. He was two hours late for
their date and then only talked about
himself. When Gloria tried to get a word
in, he pouted and acted sullen. She ended
up being home by ten o'clock. Instead of
writing her date off as a bad evening,
however, Gloria obsessed about whether
he would call again and spent too much
time discussing with a friend whether or
not to call him. Eventually she did call

him and got the cold shoulder for her troubles. Gloria's actions are an example of self-destructive behavior.

Reaching out to a man and taking an emotional risk requires great effort and concentration. Don't waste your energy on just any guy, as Gloria did. Look for men who are worth your effort, then put your energy into a man who is good to you and good for you in many ways. You'll get something back for the help you give. You wouldn't keep working at a job if you didn't get paid. So only work on a man who pays off in some way for you.

Though his beginnings be but poor and low, thank God a man can grow!
—Florence Earle Coate

~ 40 ~

*Trying to change a man who has no
interest in change is an impossible
task. I can let it go.*

Lizzie would like her boyfriend to be
more interested in her career as a publi-
cist, but he isn't. He never asks about her
day and will only listen to her talk about
her job for a few minutes before he
changes the subject.

Letitia would like Thomas to enjoy
vacations. But he's not into traveling. He
goes begrudgingly, but she knows he'd
just as soon be home.

Camille wants to know what's
troubling Manuel, but he becomes more
reluctant to talk about it the more she
asks. He doesn't like listening to
Camille's problems and has told her that
kind of talk is not his thing.

Mary Jane yearns to have William be
more romantic. She feels that sex with

him is perfunctory and wants to be seduced, to hear him say, "I love you," to have him give her flowers or ask her to a romantic dinner.

You can't force a man to be different, to love vacations or be passionate or talkative about his feelings and yours. You can say what you need, but that's all. If you can let go of thinking that somehow if you push him hard enough or try hard enough, he will change, you'll find a great burden lifted off your shoulders.

If you know how often I say to myself, to hell with everything, to hell with everybody, I've done my share, let the others do theirs now, enough, enough, enough!
—Golda Meir

~ 41 ~

Even if I can't change him,
I can change myself.

Certain personality traits of his may
never change. But you don't have to
stick with bad habits because he's not
changing his. Let's look at Joan.

Joan started to gain weight after she
began dating Sam. He liked to eat at
restaurants all the time and always
ordered large portions of food. And he
didn't like to exercise. That was bad
news for Joan. She was keeping pace with
Sam and stopped being concerned about
her weight. She let her health club mem-
bership end because Sam liked her to
stay in bed with him in the mornings.
The pounds began creeping on for both
of them and they began to wear larger
sizes. Finally, a friend suggested that
Joan come with her to Weight Watchers.
Joan was offended but woke up to the

situation. "I gave up on Sam; he's got to make his own decisions about his weight. But I started exercising. Sam complained at first when I got up early, but now he's used to it. I also cut down on my portion sizes and insisted that we stay home and eat healthy a few times a week. Sam was really moody for a while, and it turned out that he was worried that if I lost weight I would start to look for someone else. I told him I'm doing this for me. Not for a man."

Nothing can bring you
peace but yourself.
—Ralph Waldo Emerson

~ 42 ~

When my man won't work on his problems, I will detach with love.

You've screamed, you've shouted, you've cried, you've threatened, you've talked calmly, and you've come up with solutions. They don't stick. Your man won't go with you for couples therapy. Nothing changes.

It's time to detach with love. This means feeling separate from him although you're together. It doesn't mean you have to leave him. When his problem area arises, separate yourself from his actions and go on living your life as you normally would, trying to make yourself happy. If he's chronically late, make no plans with him at all where he has to arrive from somewhere else. If he refuses to consider your sexual needs, stop having sex. If he is chronically in trouble of some kind at his job or with money or with an addiction issue (cigarettes, alcohol, drugs), be politely sympathetic but do not discuss the issue with him at all. This is his problem to come to terms with. Protect yourself when necessary. You still love him, you still care about him, you can stay with him in the relationship, but when you detach you are no longer a part of his problem.

I'll lie here and learn
How, over their ground,
Trees make a long shadow
And a light sound.
—Louise Bogan

~ 43 ~

The words we use do matter.
"I feel" is the language of lasting love.

"You are the sun, the moon, the stars for me." These are words that we associate with love. But for romantic love to last, for passion to endure, you and your man need to build a foundation that will endure throughout the hard times that every couple has. The foundation is built with healthy patterns of communication, word by word. "I feel . . ." sentences are the bricks for a lasting foundation.

Your choice of words can harm disastrously, or help. You and your man always have a choice about which words to use—even when you're furious. When rage sweeps over us, we often say things we regret after the feeling passes. A marvelous first step toward changing this pattern is when you and your mate decide to try expressing your feelings instead of attacking when angry. Even if you don't succeed right away—and few people do at first—you're in there trying together.

Try this three-part communication:

- State how you feel (that's where the "I feel . . ." comes in).
- Describe what he has done to upset you. Keep it short and sweet and not too harsh, or you won't listen to each other.
- Caringly state how you want him to handle this situation differently, whether you want more foreplay in bed, for example, or for him to avoid barking orders at you when he's had a bad day at work.

You have to count on living every single day in a way you believe will make you feel good about your life.
—*Jane Seymour*

Part 3

Staying True to Yourself

~ 44 ~

When a man judges my feelings
I judge myself, too. My feelings are not
right or wrong, not good or bad.
I can stop judging my feelings or
anyone else's.

If only you could select feelings like you select a dress and wear those feelings when you wanted to. But clothing is external while feelings are buried deep. Anger, anxiety, jealousy, rage, sadness, happiness, sexual arousal—these feelings adorn us even though we'd rather throw them off our shoulders. To succeed and survive with a difficult man, you must accept and embrace all your feelings, because he won't. He will try to make you feel wrong if you're angry, might say you're foolish because you feel anxiety.

Your feelings are your guide to situations that are not healthy for you and need to change. If you try to talk yourself out of your anger, it will return anyway.

Laura felt annoyed at night when Lou collapsed in front of the TV, leaving her to make dinner and clean up even though they both worked. She convinced herself that she was spoiled to be angry, to think that he should help. This went on for about two months until one night something inside her snapped and she broke two dishes. She screamed and screamed at Lou. He was furious and hurt. After their argument wound down they spoke calmly to each other. Eventually, they worked out an arrangement whereby they would split the work. Laura resolved to pay attention to her anger sooner.

Feelings are untidy.
—Esther Hautzig

~ 45 ~

*If I play the good girl who ignores
what she feels and knows, I will lose
with a man and lose myself, too.
I don't have to be "good" any longer.*

Boys can be cut-ups, self-important, messy, and pushy, and that's fine. Women, on the other hand, are still expected to please and care for others— to be pleasant and self-effacing, never angry or demanding. Much of the reason for this lies in society's insistence on casting women in the all-nurturing, earth mother role—the supporter men can rely on and turn to, who will be there for them as they move out and up in the world, and who will ask for nothing for herself and never complain. But good, pleasant women finish last with difficult men.

Marsha always dressed immaculately and was polite and agreeable, as she had been taught at home and at her prep school. But after tirelessly working on a project at her job as a magazine production assistant, she was passed over for a promotion. In addition to her disappointments at work, Marsha was experiencing problems with her boyfriend, who repeatedly stood her up or kept her waiting. She started having crying jags that wouldn't stop. In a therapy group she learned how angry she really was and how appropriate that feeling was in her current situation. She learned how to speak up at work and to her boyfriend about his neglect. She eventually was promoted, and her boyfriend stopped keeping her waiting.

Our feelings are our most genuine
paths to knowledge.
—*Audre Lorde*

Most of the time I don't understand what I feel, so how could I be a role model for a man? But that's just my low self-esteem talking. I try to be aware of my feelings, which is more than what most men do.

Even if you are often unsure about what you feel, you, without a doubt, have had far more experience with your emotions and with nurturing than most men you know. That makes you the role model in a relationship. For example, if your man is bad at giving compliments, model it for him. If you want him to praise you, praise him. Women have been socialized to do this naturally, while some men are taught that giving compliments makes them look hen-pecked and weak. There is no more powerful teacher than an example; keep this in mind even if at first you meet with skepticism or laughter from your man in response to your praise.

There are dangers when you nurture and praise. Say only what you really feel, and don't manipulate or just make a point. Don't keep praising him or talking about your feelings unless he eventually starts to do the same. Remember that you can try giving him the words to use for compliments, or even to express his feelings, because this type of communication may be like Greek to him. Being a role model for a man doesn't mean that he will change and become like you, but the gap may narrow.

Example is not the main thing in influencing others. It is the only thing.
—Albert Schweitzer

~ 47 ~

At times I get swept away by negative feelings. But I am stronger than that. My feelings do not possess me.

"Sticks and stones may break my bones, but feelings can never harm me." With a new twist, the children's rhyme we learned to protect ourselves from bullies still holds meaning. Your feelings are important, but they can't harm you and they do not define you. Your mind is in charge, rather than your feelings. You can move beyond what you feel.

Here's an example: After ten years of marriage, Adam told Jackie he wanted a divorce. He was leaving her for another woman. The blow was devastating. Jackie felt mortally wounded, frozen, and obsessed with his new woman. She stayed in bed, kept thinking about her, cried, and felt too sick to work. After a week had passed, she woke up one day in a rage. She called a lawyer and proceeded to take action to protect herself financially and legally. Her feelings changed and she moved on. The next day she was back at work. She often feels furious or sad, but sometimes she feels free and terrific. She is in control of her life.

You are stronger than what you feel. Any negative feeling, no matter how overwhelming, will grow less powerful and will pass. So wait—you can return to being in charge of yourself and your life.

I can pardon everyone's
mistakes but my own.
—*Marcus Porcius Cato*

48

*I don't have to feel ashamed to need
the man I love or anyone else. People
ought to need each other.*

Here's Cathy's story, "I've been married
to Joseph for eight years. A couple of
months ago I developed pains in my
back. The doctor recommended I have an
MRI. The idea of sitting in one of those
tube things made me anxious, so I asked
Joseph to come with me. His response
was, 'I can't go, but don't be a baby.
Don't be so needy. You're a grown
woman for God's sake.' I was crushed."

Joseph berated and attacked Cathy.
His vicious response is a warning
signal. It alerts the listener to the fact
that Joseph is terrified of his own
dependency needs, which are probably
even stronger than Cathy's but are
hidden under layers of a "tough-guy"
defense.

Women in our society are thought of as needy, but men, who need lots of attention when they are ill, who do far worse when a relationship ends, who cannot function without secretaries and wives to bolster them, are thought of as independent. We are all "needy" in some way. We need each other to live, to love, to depend on in sickness and in health, through joy and tears. Admitting that you need others does not make you "needy." It makes you a psychologically honest and healthy person. Don't let anyone make you think otherwise.

Don't hold the sprout against the seed,
don't hold this need against me . . .
—Melanie

49

*Jealousy within reason and without
accusations is healthy. I won't abuse
or belittle my jealous feelings.*

Love and jealousy go together. From
birth on, if you perceive that anyone you
love loves another, you might feel
jealous. Problems arise when you try to
ignore your jealous feelings. Perhaps you
ignore your jealousy because you think it
is an immature reaction. Or you think
that expressing jealousy puts you in a
weak position, as if you need someone
more than he needs you. Neither of these
ideas is true. Truly secure and strong
people feel jealous, too—in fact, they feel
entitled to feel jealous and don't think
inferiority or control has anything to do
with it.

Taylor tried to suppress her jealousy
when her husband Will began to see his
two daughters from his first marriage

more often because they moved closer. Taylor felt as if Will ignored her when they were around. She also ignored her jealous feelings when Will spent an evening engrossed in conversation with a new, attractive colleague. Then Taylor developed migraine headaches. When she realized the connection, she spoke up to Will, which turned him around. He began to pay more attention to Taylor, which was better for both of them.

The "green-eyed monster" causes much woe, but the absence of this ugly serpent argues the presence of a corpse whose name is Eros [the Greek god of love].
—Minna Antrim

~ 50 ~

When I keep my needs and complaints
inside, I feel safe but also deprived.
It's worth the risk to speak up
and get more.

You're keeping your needs bottled up
because you're afraid—of his anger or
rejection or of your own anger. It's time
to take that emotional risk: to come out
of the closet where you silently suffer,
say what you feel, and ask for what you
need and want. Trust that he will
respond. Don't assume he will act like
your parents did—or the way other men
act. Believe in his love for you, even if he
sounds upset by your complaints and
requests and feelings. He needs this relationship as much as you do. He may
never have had anyone try to work out a
relationship with him before, anyone
who would put in the kind of risk and
effort that you are brave enough to do.

He will admire you and respect you in the end if you are truly motivated by one goal only—to achieve a relationship with him that is equal and fair and healthy and fun and loving for both of you. The only way to remove the impediments to that ideal is to jump the hurdle of your fear and take a risk.

Speak up for yourself,
or you'll end up a rug.
—*Mae West*

~ 51 ~

This weak, mousy state I get into around men is upsetting. But I know I can change that by getting support from people around me.

Secure women get what they want from men more often than insecure women do. Ellen says: "I used to tell a man my life story on the first date, but I don't do that anymore. I've learned to stop, look, and listen with each guy I meet. I play it much cooler now and the guys treat me better. I still find dating to be an ordeal, but this way *I* get to decide if they'll have a second date, not the other way around."

Mary Ann says: "My boyfriend does this awful thing: He mocks me in front of his friends. He'll say, 'You don't know what you're talking about,' when I talk about politics, for instance. I usually freeze up or mutter under my breath if other people are around. Later, if I yell at

him about making me look like a jerk, he
laughs it off or storms out of the house
for a couple of hours. But I'm getting too
old for this and don't want to take it anymore. He started it the other night when
we were at dinner with friends—and
I got up from the table and took a cab
home. Yesterday, when we were at a
party, I saw him grit his teeth when
I said what I thought but he kept his
mouth shut. I guess actions speak louder
than words. I found out I have strength
I didn't know I had."

The loving are the daring.
—Bayard Taylor

*I have an inner strength. I can bring
up the truth and talk about his affair.*

Most women know when their man is
having an affair or seeing someone else.
They can sense it even without hard and
fast evidence. Some women, however,
choose to ignore what they intuit—
usually, because they are afraid. Although
you might rationalize that he'll get over
this "fling," one affair may lead to
another—or even to a serious relationship. If you have a vision of a monogamous relationship with your man, you
must confront him about what he's doing
right away, or your relationship will
sooner or later end.

The strength and confidence you
have in yourself will influence him when
you say the affair has to stop. Let him
know that you are worthwhile and that
he's crazy to risk losing your love. *Never*

accept responsibility for his affair. Even if your hair is grayer, even if you've ignored him because of an all-consuming project or a new baby, it is his responsibility to speak up and say he's miserable with you *before* looking elsewhere. *Don't* go back to business as usual after he ends the affair, because the problems that caused it in the first place will not just go away. It's unlikely that he'll seek help on his own, so you *must* go for help as a couple. That should be a condition for your taking him back.

It is better to be a lion for a day
than a sheep all your life.
—Elizabeth Kenny

~ 53 ~

When I'm not getting anything from
a relationship, I will pull the reins
and stop nurturing. If I don't,
I'll be hurting myself.

You can recognize a spoiled child when you see one, but you have trouble perceiving that a grown man may be spoiled. So you keep being loving and giving, and replenish him until you are exhausted and depleted. This is a form of masochistic behavior.

Martha is an over-giver at work and at home. Her boss at the design firm where she works refuses to give her a pay increase, despite the fact that she has created many of the sketches for which her boss has taken credit. Her salary is the same as it was when she was a receptionist finishing her degree. At home, things are just as bad. Curt, her husband, is an up-and-coming lawyer, but the politics at his firm are cutthroat. Each day she listens carefully to his woes and counsels him on how to proceed. But when she asks for advice about her boss he yells, "When are you going to get a real job?" Even though Curt's salary is much higher than Martha's he refuses to kick in more than half the expenses.

It is crazy for Martha to continue helping these men. She can look for another job. She can stop counseling her husband. She can tell him she's too busy to listen to him or stay silent after he pours out his day's story. The silence will speak more than a thousand words.

Women temper men.
We have a good influence on them.
—Helen Reddy

~ 54 ~

*I deserve "positive stroking,"
even though the men I have
known have been unable to give
me compliments and nurturance.*

Positive stroking is not a physical act, but
an emotional one: the giving of praise,
admiration, "I love yous"; the offering of
a sympathetic and supportive ear. Most
men don't get this right and rarely offer
it at the moment you need it. You're
dressed up and ready to go out, for
example, and he says nothing about the
way you look. You've had a tough day at
work, and he watches TV instead of listening to you talk about why you're
upset. Even worse, he rarely says "I love
you." But you're always ready to listen to
him and say something nice. The picture
is not a flattering one for you. Your
self-esteem can drop like a stone when
you're with a man who withholds

positive stroking—especially if you go out of your way to be good to him.

Until you can teach him to give you the compliments and support you need (men *can* be taught), remember that you're not having a bad hair day, there's nothing wrong with your outfit, you are great and look terrific. He's got a problem with nurturance. Maybe his father ignored his mother; maybe his parents thought a child who is praised will become spoiled and never said nice things to him. Positive stroking is not in his repertoire. That's all it is. Find male and female friends who will tell you good things in the meantime. You deserve all the love and support you can find.

Let us crown ourselves with rosebuds,
before they be withered.
—*The Bible*

～ 55 ～

Deep down, he's no different than
I am. My intuition is clear, no matter
how he seems on the surface.

He seems so different from you, with his
walled-off behavior, rage, or silences. In
fact, you may think of him as a stronger
species. After all, you cry more than he
does. You worry more than he does. But
look deeper, and you'll find that you are
so similar emotionally as to be twins.
Women who have been with one man
a long while know that their man's
tough-guy act is only that, an act.

Keisha is always the one to complain
about service in restaurants. If she has to
wait too long for a table, she complains.
If the food is cold, she sends it back. Her
husband, Tom, tells her that she's impatient and nasty to people, but Keisha
knows this isn't true. She came up with
a plan. She and Tom met at a popular

restaurant one Friday night and were told it would be a fifteen-minute wait for a table. Forty-five minutes passed and Keisha still did not complain; she just sat and read a book. Tom looked at her strangely. After they had waited an hour, Tom jumped up. He yelled at the hostess, grabbed Keisha's hand, and stormed out saying he'd never eat there again. Keisha just smiled. She knew that, deep down, Tom was just as "impatient" as she was.

Judge a tree from its fruit;
not from the leaves.
—Euripedes

~ 56 ~

*I want to be loved by a man, faults
and all. I realize that faults can be an
asset if you learn from them. Today
I'll try to love myself just as I am.*

So you tend to bite your nails when
you're nervous. Maybe you get nasty
when you're under stress. Perhaps you
procrastinate about paying bills or
cleaning the house. Or maybe you spend
too much on clothes or could stand to
lose fifteen pounds. Is there anyone in
the world who doesn't have faults? Rich
or poor, beautiful or not? Man or
woman? Of course not; we all have them.

Admitting you have faults, and
acknowledging them, is more important
than conquering them. That hot temper
for instance. Do you apologize when it
flares up? That is the key in having a
relationship: not that the man and
woman are without faults, but that they

are willing to admit to them and work on the problems.

You want to be loved by a man as you are. Then love yourself as you are. Your extra weight is no reason to think you are unworthy of a good relationship. Because you're uncomfortable making conversation is no reason to think you are unlovable. You have big feet? So what. You hate cooking? You can send out. Make a list of your attributes, the things you like about yourself. When you find yourself focusing on your faults, think about this list instead.

Regret is an appalling waste of energy;
you can't build on it;
it's only good for wallowing in.
—Katherine Mansfield

*Monogamy in a relationship is
important. I am worth finding a
man who will be loyal to me.*

You think, "Oh, he's too smart, too
good looking, too clever to be interested in me." But he may think the
same about you. Instead of worrying
about whether or not he's interested,
what do you really think of him? Is this
a man with whom you want to have a
future? Are you deeply in love or do
you just want to be? Next you have to
believe that monogamy is the only way
you can get what you want and that
you are a valuable woman who can find
someone else if a man does not want to
commit. Only make an investment with
a man who seems ready for commitment.
A simple reality is that men are sometimes more eager to commit if they've
had trouble before in a relationship.

This often leaves men wanting to make the next relationship work.

Ellen wanted to bring up monogamy with Rob after three months of weekly dating, but she was sure he'd reject her. She thought he was too good for her. Then she heard that Rob was seeing other women. She was cold to him when she next saw him and he asked her what was going on. She told him. His reaction was totally unexpected. He said he thought she was seeing other people so he was protecting himself. Ellen and Rob were able to straighten everything out that night.

Inconsistency is the only thing in
which men are consistent.
—Horatio Smith

~ 58 ~

I don't need a man to approve
of me, as I've always thought.
I'll remind myself today that
I'm lovable the way I am.

Yolanda was searching for approval from
a man to make her feel worthwhile. She
says: "I had become a yo-yo, but I didn't
know it. Jackson, my boyfriend, was a
guitarist in a band and the best lover I
ever had. His performances were exciting
and being his girlfriend gave me status.
When I saw him, that is. When he got
around to calling me and we got together
I felt on top of the world—like I was a
queen and everyone thought I was the
greatest. But when he didn't call, I
dropped to feeling my worst. I hated
myself and thought everyone else hated
me, too. I hated everybody because I figured they didn't really like me unless I
was with him. 'Why should they like me?'

I thought. 'I'm nothing, a nobody; there's nothing about me to love, anyway.' I went up and down like this over many months, maybe a year. Then I couldn't stand it anymore. I cut myself off from Jackson, went to a codependent support group meeting with a friend, and found out I had a problem. Now I say a daily meditation that starts with, 'I am a lovable woman.' I'm starting to believe it. I won't ever again give any person the power to make me feel lovable and happy."

I conceived at least one great love in my life,
of which I was always the object.
—Albert Camus

~ 59 ~

Confidence in my own opinions is more important in the long run than a man's approval.

Maybe you've been thinking that it's more important to have your man's approval and to keep harmony in the relationship than to offer an opinion that differs from his. But what if he planned to fly a private plane in the fog and wanted you to accompany him? Say you expressed misgivings and he said, "This plane is perfectly safe. Don't you trust me?" Would you go to keep harmony, possibly risking your life? How far will you take your silence? If you feel that you must have a man's approval, it will be hard for you to disagree in words or action.

Pam played the flute as a child and had given it up until she read about a small orchestra in her town. She told her

husband she had joined the orchestra
and that she would be out once a week.
He ranted and raved about who would
make dinner and put their youngest to
bed, and even implied that she would
flirt with men. Pam reassured him and
arranged dinners for the nights she was
out. Her husband calmed down when she
remained adamant. Stand by what you
know is best. Weather the storm, and
your relationship will improve, because
you are a woman worth being with.

*As long as a woman is dependent
on a man for her self-image . . .
she will remain without any sense
of her own worth.*
—Eleanor Perry

Today I refuse to rush in to solve a man's problems because he thinks that's all I'm good for. I should be loved for who I am, not for what I do as a caretaker.

You don't want to get roped into solving your man's problems, but somehow you keep finding yourself counseling him, making the phone calls he should make for himself, making excuses for him, even bailing him out financially. Maybe you expect to get something from him in return, but you never do. So you resent the effort you've put in.

Maybe you're scared not to help him because he might get hurt or pull you down financially, too. But what you're really afraid of is that if you're not there taking care of him, he won't want you anymore. He'll find someone new.

You are worth more than the actions you take to rescue another. You deserve to be loved for who you are, for all your wonderful qualities. And if your man doesn't love you this much, do you really want to let him use you as a kind of Saint Bernard rescue service? If you answer, "Yes, I'll do what I need to keep him," then you should take time for some self-examination. Someone in your past may have given you a message that said, "I don't really love you, but I'll let you stay and will put up with you if you take care of me." Now that you're an adult woman, you can talk back to that perverse communication, "I'm not a child anymore. I'm liked for who I am, not what I do."

A watermelon that breaks open by itself tastes better than one cut with a knife.
    —Hualing Nieh

~ 61 ~

*I'm proud of my decision to give
up trying to get him to do things.
I can only control my own
words and actions.*

It may sound as if you've hit a dead end
when you have tried everything and your
relationship still is not the way you want
it. But it will not be a dead end if you
come away from all you've attempted
with a different attitude.

As Cordelia explains: "It's impossible to control anyone else, and it's bad
for me to try to do so. I say this over and
over to myself. Now I feel free, though
I'm giving up a fantasy that my boyfriend
will change. I feel a loss. Since there's
nothing I can do to improve the situation, I've let go. It's time to rest and to
start concentrating on myself."

When you think about it, there are
many ways to get your needs met apart

from through the man in your life. By digging deep inside yourself you will find the resources to make yourself happy, relaxed, and fulfilled that were there all the time. You will find that what you *expected* him to be is not really what you *needed* from him. He will feel closer to you once you've stopped trying to change him.

This time, like all times, is a very good one,
if we but know what to do with it.
—Ralph Waldo Emerson

62

I used to listen to others instead of my own intuitive voice. I now realize that my own gut feeling is a powerful tool in making decisions.

Rolanda tells us: "I was tortured by thinking my judgment was poor. Even the smallest decisions I had to make, like whether I should go to a movie or meet a friend for dinner, were an ordeal. Shopping was a nightmare, so I'd bring along a pushy friend who told me what to buy. Then I'd get home and hate what I bought. When it came to Ben, my boyfriend, of course I doubted my judgment. There was a little voice in my head saying he was hiding something from me. But a friend told me I was nuts, that I was lucky to be with him. Then I found out Ben was married and had a child in another state.

"I didn't trust my intuition, because my parents had been too overprotective.

They told me what to do about everything and never let me make any decisions. 'You're too young, too flighty,' they would say. I believed them. But now that I know my intuition was right about Ben, I've started listening to my gut feelings. If I relax and don't pressure myself, what I need and believe comes to me."

Other people's opinions are helpful at times, but they are only opinions—not facts. Sit in a quiet place and listen— eventually you'll hear that still, small voice that is your intuition.

If a woman carries her own lantern,
she need not fear darkness.
—Hasidic saying

63

Like a quiet pond in the summer, other people look so perfect to me. But below the surface, life and death struggles are being fought. I won't be ashamed of my life's struggles.

Marian and Ted have big arguments. They've only been married a year and Marian worries that she made a mistake in marrying Ted. Sure, they make up pretty quickly, and nobody holds a grudge. But it has gotten so intense that they went to see a marriage counselor. Meanwhile, the other couples Marian knows all seem idyllic. Her friend Alison told her how ecstatic she is that she and her husband Eric never fight. They bike, hike, camp, and go to craft shows together. Marian felt like she was damaged in comparison. Six months later, however, Marian got a call from a distraught Alison: Eric was having an affair; what should she do?

"Thou doth gloat too much" is a phrase to keep in mind when a woman tells you how fabulous her relationship is. Your friend is probably scared of conflict with her man for some reason stemming from her childhood and has to paint a perfect picture to keep herself calm. Maybe she thinks that if things aren't perfect, there won't be anything at all. You never know what complexities may exist in someone else's relationship—or what deals are made between these apparently perfect couples. Many of these deals are not ones you'd accept. You're honestly dealing with problems—give yourself credit, not a hassle.

I find the great thing in this world is not so much where we stand, as in what direction we are moving.
—Oliver Wendell Holmes

64

*I don't like to look at myself because
then I think I have to change. But
"just observing" is the real way that
change begins.*

Every parent knows you can't force a
child to be toilet-trained or go to sleep
or eat his or her vegetables. As we get
older, however, we think we should be
able to force ourselves into new patterns
that are good for us. But there's no
forcing change.

Observing yourself is the first step
toward change. Let's say you're usually
too passive around your man and he
pushes you around (emotionally
speaking) like Archie Bunker pushed
Edith in the comedy *All in the Family*.
When Edith realized she was a wimp,
she felt compelled to battle Archie every
second to make everything different
immediately. These forced changes didn't

last long. Neither of them was ready for life to be that different overnight.

All you need to do to put change in motion is to start observing yourself—and him. This requires you to believe that your mind on its own, without much effort on your part, will make change as you are ready. Changes that are subtle to begin with will last. During this process, it is important to refrain from self-criticism. That means no self-attack, no impatience with yourself, no putting yourself down, no blaming yourself (I "shoulda" said this, I "coulda" done that). "No one pushes the river," as the Buddhists say, "it flows just fine by itself."

As I walk,
As I walk,
The Universe is walking with me.
—Navajo rain dance ceremony

65

Even though I'm ready to leave this man, I can use my strength and make sure he knows what he could do to keep me. I can leave at any time.

Many a relationship has ended before a verbal shot has been fired—before either of you has had a chance to argue, to be angry, or to work out a compromise. When there's a problem, you owe it to yourself and to him to tell him what's wrong so he has a chance to get it right. Maybe he should know without you telling him. Or perhaps you have told him before how unhappy you are. But some difficult men won't hear you unless the door is open and you say you're on your way out unless he makes a change. That's the way it is.

Think about your anger. Let's say you have one foot out the door, that you're so fed up you don't want to bother trying to work things out anymore. You'll have to take this one on faith—it's worth it to pause for a moment. Take a deep breath and let your man know how close he is to losing you. You can always leave after that. And if you do decide to break up, you'll feel better later on knowing you tried everything. Your life will feel cleaner, your vision of what you want with a man will be clearer, you will know positively that you could not get what you needed from this man.

Courage is the price life exacts
for granting peace.
—Amelia Earhart

Part 4

Caring for
Your Sexual Self

~ 66 ~

*Whether a man finds me sexy is too
important to me. It's like I'm addicted
to feeling sexy and having sex. I can
get control of this when I'm ready.*

Chocolate is rich and delicious but best
enjoyed in moderation and as part of a
generally healthy diet. The same could be
said about sex. When sex becomes your
raison d'être, your reason for living, it
becomes an addiction that can have
serious consequences. By placing too
much emphasis on sex you can end up
selling yourself short.

Let's look at Ariel. She is every
man's dream in many ways. She's a
dancer who projects a sensuality that is
emphasized by the provocative clothing
she wears. It seems as if there's an endless supply of men ready to have sex with
her. Ariel's flattered by this attention and
ends up sleeping with the men she meets

more often than not. In a "bad" week, when she doesn't meet anyone new, she immediately questions her attractiveness. She feels anxious when she doesn't have sex, as if her identity is in jeopardy and no one loves her. Ariel has other interests she could share in a relationship. She paints and is an animal rights activist. But no one knows about this.

Beneath this sexual acting out Ariel is hiding strong insecurities about being loved. If she gets help to deal with her insecurities, she will eventually find a man who will appreciate all of her qualities.

In sexual intercourse it's quality not quantity that counts.
—Dr. David Reuben

*Real intimacy with a man is scary if
I think about it. All my old fears—
and new ones—come up. I can get
what I want if I face the fear.*

Fear is a big impediment to taking risks,
whether you're considering scaling a
mountain or asking your man to touch
you in a certain way. Many of us feel fear
when we get close to someone. You're
afraid you'll be abandoned or hurt, or
you may even be afraid the relationship
will go well. Yet the real problem is not
fear, but what you and your man do to
avoid feeling afraid.

You may avoid taking the risks you
need to take in order to get what you
want because of the fear your man will
stop loving you. Yet the likelihood is that
although he might not do what you ask,
consider making a change, or even talk to
you about an issue, he'll stay around.

Joyce told Richard she wanted to stay at a hotel the next time they visited his mother. Although she hadn't said anything negative about his family, Richard was outraged. He called her a princess and wouldn't talk to her for three days. When she brought it up again, he barked an angry, "Do what you want," and gave her the silent treatment for another two days. But at Thanksgiving when they made the visit and stayed at a hotel, Joyce and Richard both relaxed, enjoying the time away from his critical mother. Richard finally admitted that he liked the new arrangement.

You never find yourself
until you face the truth.
—Pearl Bailey

~ 68 ~

*I can overcome the fear of speaking up
when I'm in bed with a man. I have a
right to take care of myself.*

Sex is the toughest terrain for talking
because feelings like shame and performance anxiety stifle you. Even if he's sensitive, no man can know where you like to
be touched. If you don't speak up, the
dissatisfaction will eat away at your relationship. And, physically speaking, worse
can happen to you if you don't speak up
about the use of condoms—at least until
you're sure about a man's commitment
and his health.

Beverly met Frank, a friend of a
friend, at a party. He had a great sense of
humor and was warm and interested in
her. After kissing in a back room, they
left the party and went to her apartment.
Beverly was nervous about the condom
issue. She forced herself to ask Frank

directly about using one. He snickered and said, "I can make sure I'm out of there before anything happens." Beverly told him that that wasn't the issue. Frank said he had a clean bill of health; Beverly said she still wanted him to use a condom. Frank said the conversation was a turnoff—and then left.

Beverly was furious but felt awful. She called a friend, who told her how terrific she was for standing up for herself. Speak up. Protect yourself. And ask for what you need in bed.

If sex and creativity are . . . seen by dictators as subversive activities, it's because they lead to the knowledge that you own your own body (and with it your own voice), and that's the most revolutionary insight of all.
—Erica Jong

~ 69 ~

*The idea of asking for anything during sex
scares me. But even if he gets upset,
I'll be fine. I'm no longer a little girl.*

We all tend to get a little childish when
we're in a relationship. Consider men
who call their wives "mother" (we've
even heard presidents do this). Therapists have a name for this: it's called
regression, going backward emotionally.
But if something's going on in your sex
life that you don't like but haven't put a
stop to, you're regressing and it's a sign
that you should take a pause. It's true
that anything's okay between two consenting adults as long as no one gets
hurt, but the key word here is *consenting.*
You're no longer a child who must do as
she's told. Don't consent out of fear that
he'll go find someone else.

For years, Cheryl had reluctantly
agreed to be tied up by her husband

during sex, even though she hated it. She never got hurt, but the act damaged her pride. Cheryl ended up joining a women's support group and finally got up the courage to tell her husband she didn't want to do it anymore. She expected him to be furious—even to leave her. None of that happened, although for the next year, they had sex infrequently. Finally, she got him to go for counseling with her. Their sex life has picked up and Cheryl is feeling sexy for the first time. Her husband seems like a new person.

It doesn't matter what you do in the bedroom as long as you don't do it in the street and frighten the horses.
—Mrs. Patrick Campbell
(Beatrice Stella Tanner)

～ 70 ～

*Sexual fantasies are exciting and fun,
but I won't let them get in the way
of what I need in reality.*

Fantasies can do a lot to keep a relationship passionate and alive, even if you keep your fantasies to yourself. Lila would think about a boyfriend from high school when she was with her husband: thinking about having sex in a parked car as a high school senior seemed more exciting now that she was older. Sometimes she'd think about a neighbor. But she knew that if she told her husband about her fantasies he'd feel threatened—as if she'd actually cheated. Fantasies should never be shared unless you both clearly want this. Fantasies that remain in your mind are never a betrayal or hurtful.

Fantasies brought out into the open without regard for your partner's feelings are misused and can end a relationship.

This happened to Gwen. After a few months of seeing Dan, he revealed to her that he liked sadomasochistic sex— simply put, tying her up or being tied up himself—even some spanking. He showed Gwen the paraphernalia that he used in sex. She was upset and let him know that she wasn't into his fantasy. That was the end of the relationship. But Gwen was strong and felt good that she had not been coerced into performing an act she didn't want to just to keep this man. She was understandably angry; he hadn't really cared about her—only about whether she'd be willing to play his game.

If one is lucky, a solitary fantasy can totally transform one million realities.
—Maya Angelou

~ 71 ~

*I can act confident during sex even if
I don't feel that way. I am strong
enough to ask for what I want.*

Your feelings are not facts, as the 12-step
programs say. They're just tapes that
replay over and over in your head. You
say to yourself, "I'm not good-looking
enough. He'll think I'm fussy and com-
plaining if I say, 'Please touch me here,'
or 'I like it this way,' or 'I need more foreplay.' He'll get angry or not call again. Or
we won't have sex anymore. Other
women are better than I am in bed."

Now think of yourself as having a
body double, like in the movies. Your
double looks exactly like you, talks like
you, and has the same wit and intelligence, but she feels confident and entitled to be treated well by any man she
goes to bed with. She isn't any more
entitled than you, but she believes that

she has a right to ask for what she needs. She does not attack herself if a man responds badly, if he disappears and doesn't call gain. Your body double knows she did the right thing when she asked him to please her, too (and to use condoms). She knows she was willing and ready to offer pleasure. She knows that if a man doesn't call again, then he has a problem. Your confident body double knows this. You should, too.

The important thing is not what they think of me, but what I think of them.
—Queen Victoria

When I'm disappointed with sex,
blaming myself or the man won't get
me anywhere. I can work out the
problem without criticizing anyone.

Considering how orgasmic, picturesque,
and simple the media make sex look,
it's easy to feel disappointed by the
reality of your sexual partner. Our
sexual expectations are often unrealisti-
cally high. Maria, for example, predicted
two days of passion during a weekend
away with Joshua, her new man, and
actually brought two boxes of condoms
with her. Their one and only attempt at
sex was unsatisfying and doomed to
failure, because they had both made
themselves a wreck with their outra-
geous expectations.

A man may, in fact, not respond to
you. Women are often disappointed
because men ignore their needs. Don't

blame yourself. Speak up about what you want in bed.

Disappointment about sex can rekindle thoughts of past disappointments in our lives, making the feeling overly intense. You expect that sex will make everything better and make all your dreams and fantasies come true. It's not possible. Sex can never make up for losses in our lives, frustrations about jobs, despair about the future, problems with a child. Be alert so that you don't blame a man for your disappointment in the bedroom and that a man doesn't blame you if his unrealistic fantasy didn't come true. Blame has no place in a sexual relationship.

I shall stay the way I am
Because I do not give a damn.
—*Dorothy Parker*

~ 73 ~

I'll try to remember that sex is not the place to "get it right" or to be perfect.

Olivia is a corporate lawyer with a big firm. She's on her way to becoming a partner. Rick, her fiancé, is an equally successful lawyer. Their apartment is large and modern, and remains largely empty, as they carefully fill it with abstract art and sculpture. Olivia admits she's a perfectionist, that she will examine every detail of a case. Rick's even worse. He fired three painters before he found one he believed could paint their apartment just the way he wanted. It's not surprising that their sex life is not exactly a passion pit. "It's okay," Olivia says evenly. Exactly twice a week before they go to sleep, Rick will kiss Olivia gently and attempt foreplay for about five minutes. Then they will have intercourse in the traditional position.

This couple thinks sex is like a law school assignment. But there is no right argument or decision that will be handed to them about their private nightly ritual. All their daytime postures and rules can be thrown out the window. Rick and Olivia should know that anything goes as long as they both freely agree to it. If Olivia tries to loosen up their sex life, however, she will have to be careful so that Rich won't feel criticized. Perhaps they could start by watching erotic movies or reading *The Joy of Sex*. This should help to take away the feeling that their sex life is open to judgment.

Really, sex and laughter do go very well together, and I wondered—and I still do—which is the more important.
—Hermione Gingold

74

*Harsh self-criticisms echo in
my head when it comes to sex. I must
remember that I cannot do sex badly.
It is not an exam.*

When Georgina was a child and asked
questions about death, her body, where
babies came from, or anything else that
made her mother uncomfortable, her
mother called her "stupid." Georgina
stopped asking questions by the time she
was four. Now, with her boyfriend
Gordon, she is frozen when it comes to
sex. She loves him and is turned on by
his body, but in bed she feels panicky and
helpless. In fact, Georgina has lots of
sexual fantasies and questions about sex
and about what Gordon would like in
bed, but she subconsciously believes she
is stupid and wrong in what she thinks.
She is sure that Gordon would respond
to her questions the way her mother did.

So she is quiet and passive in bed. Gordon says she's "remote." He's worried that she either doesn't like him sexually or that she's "frigid." Since Gordon is also insecure, he's not talking about the problem.

Because Georgina is *aware* that harsh criticisms from her childhood have harmed her (she may also be retaining critical messages from teachers, religious figures, family friends, or siblings), she has a chance to replace them with a different tape—one that says she is smart, sexy, and free.

Girls are taught from childhood that any exhibition of sexual feeling is unwomanly and intolerable.
—Mary Scharlieb

75

I'll watch out for "sexual thralldom"—
feeling helpless and dependent on the
man I'm with. I am the same strong,
independent woman I have always been.

Freud coined the term "sexual
thralldom"—as when a woman feels
childishly dependent on a man because
she's sleeping with him. Although
women can experience sexual thralldom
in varying degrees, for some, it can be
paralyzing.

Lorraine owns and runs a TV production house and is doing incredibly
well. The business grosses a few million a
year. Lorraine has never lacked confidence
or ideas to make her business grow. But
you would not recognize her with Vernon.
She met him a year ago and he has since
moved into her place. Vernon makes
nightly demands on Lorraine to have sex.
When Lorraine has said no, even if she is

sick, he has threatened to leave her or see other women. She feels scared of either possibility and so no longer refuses him. Lorraine feels ashamed of her cowardice, but she is in the grip of sexual thralldom and feels that she has no control over the situation. Her own father was violent when angry, and Vernon's sexual aggression feels violent to her. It makes her feel like a child again instead of the incredibly independent woman she is. Lorraine needs to tell herself that she is no longer a child, that Vernon is not her father, and that she can—and maybe should—kick him out.

No star is lost we once have seen,
We always may be what we
might have been.
—Adelaide A. Proctor

~ 76 ~

Lovemaking should always be
for mutual pleasure, not a bribe to
keep a man with me. I'm worth
more than that.

The first time that Janice made love to
Brad just to keep him happy, she
thought, "I can fake it just this once."
The next time, she thought he was too
interested in another woman at a party.
When they got home, she made sure to
satisfy him with oral sex. After a while,
Janice stopped seeing lovemaking as a
way that they could both experience
pleasure and began thinking of it as a
tool to keep Brad happy. She worried that
she wasn't attractive enough and thought
that she might be able to keep him
around with sex. A year later, Brad
decided he needed more space and left.

It never pays to compromise your
values when it comes to sex. If a man is

going to leave, no amount of sex will keep him—and really, why would you want to bother with a man who is so shallow and unable to be giving? If a man is not willing to consider or accommodate a woman's sexual needs, he should be looking for a paid professional, not a relationship.

You mustn't force sex to do the work of love or love to do the work of sex— that's quite a thought, isn't it?
—Mary McCarthy

~ 77 ~

Chasing a man for sex when he is being withholding is like trying to cuddle a snarling tiger. It's an invitation to disaster. I don't want to get hurt.

Marlene likes sex. But Anthony, her husband of two years, is in a new, stressful job and has lost interest in making love. "Not tonight, honey," was his familiar response. Marlene got more upset as the weeks went on. She tried renting X-rated movies but Anthony just asked her, "What kind of crap are you watching?" Then she tried wearing sexy underwear, but Anthony ignored her. Finally, she got angry and began asking him, "What's wrong with you? Is there someone else? Are we ever having sex again?" By the second night of this, Anthony had had enough and he turned on her. "What's with you? You sound like a nymphomaniac. You don't have orgasms much, anyway. What's the difference? It wasn't that great to begin with."

Marlene was devastated; she believed Anthony meant everything he had said. What she didn't realize is that when men withdraw sexually, they are usually confused about something and don't know why. Anthony is scared and worried. When Marlene got angry, he felt criticized for his lack of sexual performance, and so he attacked her in return. In similar situations, you should try to speak to your man about the issue without anger and stay strong despite his reaction. It might be necessary for the two of you to see a therapist or counselor.

If you have enough fantasies,
you're ready, in the event that
something happens.
—*Sheila Ballantyne*

A man can be so self-centered in bed that I just want to tell him off! But this could end up in a power struggle that I don't want. Caring requests are the only way.

Power struggles start in the family—from toilet training continuing right on up to curfews. Lydia fought with her father, who had a quick temper. Now she's with Charlie, who easily takes offense during sex if Lydia asks him to change position or to touch her in one place rather than another. When this happens, Charlie will withdraw altogether and leave the bed. Lydia argues with him a lot about this and will often end up sleeping in another room. Having grown up in an army family, Charlie has lots of control issues. Lydia also has control issues, however, and threatens to leave Charlie all the time.

Sexual struggles usually mask feelings of sadness and insecurity about whether you're lovable or a good enough partner in bed. And sex often provides nurturance and tenderness you didn't get as a child. Lydia's anger and sense of urgency about sex are adding to Charlie's control issues. For Lydia, backing off, trying a softer approach, and investigating why the two of them seem to prefer fighting over making love in a satisfying way will lessen the struggle.

Sex is never an emergency.
—Elaine Pierson

~ 79 ~

I'll remember that a man may feel
as sexually inadequate as I do;
he's just not going to say it.

Brian was the kind of guy women looked
at on the beach. Patty was proud to be
seen with him. She'd had a few dates
with Brian that had ended up with a
passionate kiss and some petting, but
that was as far as it had gone. Patty was
invited to a party and asked Brian to go.
After the party, they had engaged in
the same type of kissing and groping,
then Brian left. Patty never heard from
him again.

Although Patty had always consid-
ered herself attractive, when Brian didn't
call she decided her legs weren't shapely
enough, that she hadn't turned him on.
For several days she walked around
feeling frumpy and awful. One day, she
complained to a friend about how she

felt. As Patty told her story, the friend started laughing. She knew two women who had also dated Brian and who had stopped hearing from him just as suddenly. But one of the women had found out from a male friend that Brian was a virgin. He'd never slept with any of his dates; the bodybuilding was just a big cover-up.

Few men will admit they feel sexually inadequate. Don't wind up feeling it for them.

Love's like the measles;
we all have to go through it.
—Jerome K. Jerome

~ 80 ~

I'm willing to figure out how his parents got along—sexually and otherwise. Whatever happened at his home can happen in our bed.

Trevor was passionate when Rosie met him, and they had sex often. Then they got married. Rosie noticed a change in Trevor on their honeymoon. He was cooler in bed. Sex between them finally stopped. Rosie was distraught and angry; she felt she had been duped. But Trevor hadn't withdrawn from Rosie on purpose—in fact, he didn't realize he was behaving any differently. He was unconsciously living in the past.

Before Trevor's parents divorced, they had slept in separate bedrooms. His mother had occasionally slept with Trevor. Once Rosie became his wife and part of his family, she began to remind him of his mother. The little boy in

Trevor knows he shouldn't touch his mother, so he's staying away from Rosie. Rosie should go to a couples counselor with Travor if he's willing to go. In the meantime, she can maintain a distance from Trevor. She might ask him if he can identify specific ways she acts like his mother, and she should stop "mothering" him if she's doing that (doing his laundry, making his dinners, etc.). She should also emphasize the ways in which she is different from his mother. He may get angry, but it will help him snap out of the past.

The fact is that heterosexual sex for most people is in no way free of the power relations between men and women.
—Deirdre English and
Barbara Ehrenreich

81

*Like a tree struggling to stay rooted
in hurricane winds, I must hold
on tightly to my belief in the
possibility of a warm, sexual,
loving, reciprocal relationship.*

Bret's idea of exciting sex was to have
Gloria perform oral sex on him or to have
intercourse where, after a few thrusts, he
would climax. "You are wonderful," he
would say as he rolled over and went to
sleep. But Gloria was frustrated. If she
quietly asked Bret to make love back to
her, he would become angry, get in a huff,
and act as if he were the injured party.
For a week, he would treat her coldly,
without the consideration he usually dis-
played. "Other women have been happy
with me; what's wrong with you?" he
would say. Gloria, like most women,
thinks there's a lot that's wrong with her.
But since she had had better lovers, and

since she had read a lot about satisfying sex, she knows he has a problem.

Gloria was willing to teach Bret and withstand his coldness. "I love you and want to be with you," she would tell him, "but sex is giving and taking." And then she would tell him what she wanted. Although Bret was silent and tense for a while, she stayed calm and loving. Eventually, Bred did become more giving, and Gloria praised him as if he were the best lover on earth.

I doubt whether any girl would be satisfied with her lover's mind if she knew the whole of it.
—Anthony Trollope

Part 5

Coping with Your Anger
(and His)

82

*A perfect couple is not what
I imagined it to be. Perfect couples
argue and allow room for change.
In this kind of couple,
I'll have space to be myself.*

Many of us still believe in the old-
fashioned concept of a "perfect" couple:
If you love each other, you are always in
complete agreement and do everything
together. Sandra tried to be perfect in
Todd's eyes, which she thought meant
being just like him. When she and Todd
moved in together, she stopped seeing
her friends and only saw his. She agreed
with every item Todd purchased to deco-
rate their apartment. When they went to
the movies, he chose. Sandra gave up
her chorus practice so she could be
home with Todd and took up skiing
because Todd liked it. She went along to
basketball games, even though she was

the only woman in the group. One day Todd announced he was leaving to get his own place. He said he needed space and felt confined. Sandra was heart-broken and confused.

Sandra had twisted herself into whatever perfect shape she thought would keep Todd. That never works. Redefine perfection as being resilient and allowing for arguments and differences between two people. You have a right to your opinions, your way of life, your needs. He has a right to his. If he can't take differences, you don't need him. Healthy relationships need constructive differences.

"The point is," Evelyn said, "we're taught that we have to be perfect. Like objects in a museum, not people. People don't have to be perfect, only objects do."
—Judith Rossner

~ 83 ~

My preconceived beliefs about
arguing may not be true or helpful.
I'll keep an open mind.

The number one fallacy about arguing: You have to give in if you see the other person's point of view. Just because you understand where your man is coming from doesn't mean that he's right. Your man might say he earns most of the money, he works long hours, and he's tired, and that's why he doesn't do much around the house or watch the kids. You can see his point but still hold your position that he needs to do more with the kids and help keep the house running. When you give credence to his point of view, he feels appreciated, less angry, and more willing to cooperate. When he does the same for yours, you'll each be more willing to work the situation out.

The number two fallacy: You can't be angry if you see his point of view. This is a very destructive belief to hold onto. For example, Toni let her hair go gray. Then her husband had an affair with a much younger woman. Toni said she couldn't be angry, because she could understand that her husband needed someone who looked younger. How ridiculous. Of course she can, and ought to, be angry with him.

Repressing anger because of either of these false beliefs destroys communication and weakens you physically and emotionally.

*A ship in port is safe, but that's not
what ships are built for.*
—Grace Murray Hopper

*Harsh winds of anger blow even in
loving relationships. When I shut
down to a man's real anger, I'm
feeling scared or defensive.*

Georgia tells us, "Kyle says I don't listen to his opinion. But when he gets angry—about how much money I spend, for example—I get in a daze. Maybe I yell, maybe I cry. I sleep on the couch that night. It doesn't matter what he's angry about. I hear that tone and I go away."

Kyle has a right to feel angry. It doesn't sound as if he's attacking Georgia—just defending his point of view. Georgia needs to build up her confidence—and her tolerance—for Kyle's anger. If she were more confident, she would be able to really hear his reasons for being angry instead of falling apart. They could have a reasonable discussion about how to resolve the ongoing conflict.

Don't expect your man to act sweet all the time because his anger makes you anxious. Anger is a normal and healthy expression of conflict and is energizing to a relationship. After the two of you get things that are bothering you off your chest, you'll be able to hear each other better.

It is the disease of not listening . . .
that I am troubled withal.
—William Shakespeare

~ 85 ~

I can't tell the difference between normal anger and verbal abuse, but that can change. I'll learn to recognize mistreatment.

Anger always happens between two lovers, but verbal abuse does not have to happen. You may be so used to hearing your man criticize you or yell at you, however, that you don't recognize this behavior as mistreatment. Consider the following examples:

Lawrence is a quiet guy, unless he's had a few drinks—then he gets loud and nasty. "Who the hell are you to tell me I'm wrong?" he says to his wife, pointing his finger in her face repeatedly, when she disagrees with him about the best route home. "Just shut up. You're not smart enough to tell me anything." This is verbal abuse.

"What are you, some kind of princess? Earn more money and pay for your own clothes. You think this is a free ride? Huh? Huh?" Neil stands over Rachel, who wants to disappear. She's glad the kids are sleeping and can't hear this. She's exhausted from making dinner and taking care of the two toddlers. How exactly does Neil expect her to work harder? This is emotional abuse.

Mild or strong criticism can be abusive. "You're so dumb. What the hell is wrong with you?" Cursing at another is abusive.

If your man attacks you emotionally, say nothing and get away from him. And go for some counseling to help yourself.

The question is not what a man can scorn, or disparage, or find fault with, but what he can love, and value, and appreciate.
—*John Ruskin*

*Sometimes I take his bad behavior
and verbal assaults because
I understand him. That's destructive.
I must always protect myself.*

Caroline has been married to Jared for
two years. They both have stressful jobs:
Jared manages a software company, and
Caroline is a clothing buyer. Caroline
gets dinner together most nights. For a
week, Jared found fault with Caroline
and the dinner every night. First she got
defensive, then she got angry, then she
got quiet, and then she felt depressed.
After a few days, a friend and colleague
of Jared's happened to call and Caroline
found out that an important product at
Jared's company had done badly and
Jared had been held responsible. Jared
continued to be critical and mean, and
Caroline continued to take his abuse
because she thought she ought to

understand how terrible he felt. Meanwhile she felt awful.

Just because you're smart and know that his criticism is a sign of his own unhappiness doesn't mean you should be a doormat or garbage pail. Caroline can ask Jared, "Are you being critical and awful to me because you're upset about work? I'm hurt and angry that you're taking your feelings out on me instead of talking about what's really bothering you. I'm willing to hear about it." If Jared continues to pick on her, Caroline should leave the room—even leave the house and meet a friend—until he gets himself under control.

A dame that knows the ropes isn't likely to get tied up.
—Mae West

~ 87 ~

*I won't be diminished by a man's
anger or swept away by my own.
My intelligent, calm voice is stronger
than anger, and it will give me
the answers I need.*

Two guidelines to follow when your man
is angry—don't take any action at that
moment, and don't take to heart what he
says when he's angry. Listen to how Kate
handled a problem.

"Bob has two daughters from his
first marriage. We all get along pretty
well, but Bob and I need private time.
He gives them his full attention when
they're with us, and I become kind of a
third wheel. Bob told me we should all
go to Europe together for a month of
vacation. I said I didn't think that was a
good idea. He blew up and called me a
selfish bitch and several other choice
names. I yelled back, too, and said he

was insensitive to me. I said he didn't care about me, that he was scared of his kids, etc. It became a screaming match. Afterwards, though, I did come to better understand his point of view. After we had both calmed down, I apologized and so did he. Then I came up with a plan: two weeks with his girls, two weeks alone while they're on a teen tour. He was thrilled and said that would be more fun for everyone."

Each of you can become swept away by anger that leaves as fast as it comes. Apologies afterward are helpful so that you can both move on and clear the air. Make sure to let go of your anger before making any decisions or taking any actions.

Many a man who has known himself
at ten forgets himself utterly
between ten and thirty.
—Catherine Drinker Bowen

~ 88 ~

*I'll try to remember that although a
man is angry at me, it's not my fault.*

The problem with difficult men who
have the bad habit of attacking with
their anger is that they have no appropriate way to express this feeling. You
certainly don't want to be verbally
attacked and should never put yourself
in physical danger. So how can you make
space for a man you care about to express
his conflicts with you? Encourage him
through "parallel talking" to discuss the
problem when things are calm. Don't say
very much.

Elaine, for example, knows that
deep down Paul is a nice guy, but at a
party with her friends he was obnoxious
to everyone. He had not wanted to go to
the party at all, but she'd coaxed him to
come with her. She was angry at him, but
she also felt bad about the situation.

They had a date for that Saturday and over dinner she tried parallel talking. She said, "If it were me, I would have been angry about going to a party with your friends, where nobody seemed to care I was there. Did you feel that way?" Paul opened up immediately.

You can make space inside you to do this by thoroughly believing that there is nothing wrong with you, and that the intense part of his anger is not now, and has never been, because of you.

In passing . . . I would like to say that
the first time Adam had a chance,
he laid the blame on a woman.
—Lady Nancy Astor

It is always bad for me if I try to talk to a man when he is raging, sarcastic, nasty, or critical. I will remind myself today to walk away.

Talking to your man when he is being verbally abusive provides him with a secondary gain, in that he is rewarded for putting you down by gaining your attention. Deprive him of attention and he will get the message clearer than through anything you could say to him—that you won't put up with this behavior. Connie lived with Timothy's explosions for five years. They both worked, but when he got home he might start yelling, "This place is a pigsty. You're as much of a slob as your mother. Do I have to do everything around here?" He might throw things around as he yelled or slam a door so hard that plates would fall off a shelf and break.

Connie tried reasoning with him. Sometimes, she would yell back and they'd have a real screaming match. Nothing changed Timothy's behavior. One day a friend called and overheard Timothy yelling at Connie. She urged Connie to take action. The next time Timothy screamed, Connie put on her coat and went out for a walk. When she returned, Timothy looked at her sheepishly and apologized. Connie finally realized that the verbal abuse had never been her fault! No one has a right to talk to you that way. Reasoning with an irrational man will only hurt, not help, your situation.

If we do not change our direction, we are likely to end up where we are headed.
    —*Chinese proverb*

~ 90 ~

*I am not the cause of a man's violence,
but there are steps I must take to
protect myself if he becomes violent.
No one can change a violent man
except the man himself.*

There is nothing you do that makes your
man violent—no matter what he says. He
came to you with that potential because
of his family background. You just chose
him. One act of violence should be
enough for you to take action to protect
yourself. (An act of violence is the use of
a person's body to express anger against
you. An act of violence can take the form
of throwing items, pushing, shoving,
grabbing, hitting, punching, the use of a
weapon, or even threats of violence.)

Protecting yourself may mean leaving
your man . . . but it must also mean immediately seeking counseling for yourself and,
if necessary, a police order of protection.

If you decide to stay with a violent man, you must find out why you are willing to do so. The reasons are in your past as well as your present. You must protect yourself by figuring out how to stay out of his way when he's in that mood and ready for a fight. Since he can't tolerate normal arguments with an exchange of opinions, you need to learn to walk away from disagreements quickly. Don't try to convince him or prove a point. Leave the house to get away from his anger. Give up trying to get him to change. Work on changing yourself so that you don't need him. If you have decided to stay with him for now, these are essential life-saving steps you must take.

Women who set a low value on themselves make life hard for all women.
—Nellie McClung

~ 91 ~

*I'll use a mental image, like a red flag,
to help me stop getting involved in
useless fighting. It's not my job to
make a man see it my way.*

When a man becomes irrational in words
or actions, something has activated a lifelong pattern within him. Leave the scene
if you can't detach from what he's saying.
When you are detached, you will be able
to look at this man's life and know where
these "crazy" actions, words, or feelings
came from. Don't tell a man his feelings
sound crazy. That will scare him and
infuriate him further.

Howard, for example, is a sports
writer with tight deadlines. He procrasti-
nates about starting his work, then ends
up staying up all night before a deadline
and is wiped out the next day. This happens a few times a week. Marla, his girlfriend, tried reasoning with him about

his behavior and tried to get him to start work earlier. They would end up in a fight; Howard would accuse Marla of "bossing him around."

So Marla has started to "red flag" herself. She says nothing to Howard about his work, goes to sleep when she is ready, and ignores his exhaustion the next day. Until Howard wants to change his self-destructive behavior, there's nothing she can do except to reassure herself that his behavior has nothing to do with her and to keep enjoying her own life.

It is with our passions as it is with fire and water, they are good servants, but bad masters.
—Sir Roger L'Estrange

~ 92 ~

Speaking up about his behavior
can get me upset. But no matter
how angry I am, I won't make
any decisions in that moment.
If I do, I'll regret them later.

How would you feel if you were on a
plane and overheard the pilot and copilot
yelling at each other, then heard the pilot
announce in an agitated voice over the
loudspeaker that he was landing the
plane? You'd probably be a nervous
wreck, because you wouldn't think the
pilot was capable of good judgment at
the moment.

Now let's say you're furious,
because the man you're dating didn't call
all week and when he finally did call
you'd already made plans. Or he flirted
with your friend at a party and ignored
you. So you begin telling him how angry
you are, and as you do so you become

more and more furious. Before you know it, you're breaking up with him. Don't crash-land your plane. Express your feelings, but never make a decision to break up—or run back and make up with a man—when you are very upset. Give yourself the gift of time. Calm down. Talk it over with someone you trust. You'll be amazed at the difference a day makes. Your attitude about the event may change completely.

The greatest revolution of our generation is the discovery that human beings, by changing the inner attitudes of their minds, can change the outer aspects of their lives.
—William James

93

*I can only control what I say to a man
and how I act. I cannot control how he
responds or if he responds at all.*

Niki says: "I didn't believe in the truth of
this affirmation for a very long time. I
thought if I kept at the man in my life, I
would be able to change him. Daniel can
be so cold and distant, and I really need
warmth and conversation. So I'd try to
get him to talk to me about his day.
Then I'd try to talk about my day. His
one-word responses infuriated me, so
we'd end up in a fight. By the end of the
fight, I'd feel terrible about calling him
names and would end up apologizing. The
same interchange would take place over
and over again. Sometimes I'd give up for
a while, but I'd always end up trying to
get him to talk more and getting angry.

"Finally, I got fed up and gave up
trying. I couldn't stand the way I sounded

and felt when I yelled at him. Self-respect is important, too. When I stopped trying to get him to open up, two important changes occurred. The first was weird: I felt really alone and depressed. It was so quiet when we were together. I felt like someone had died. I started calling friends and got involved in church groups, which helped a lot. The other change was that Daniel started asking me how my day was. He began paying a little more attention to what I said and made an effort to talk the more I stayed quiet around him. I feel closer to him now. Most important, I respect myself now."

Usually passion wants to grab and yank.
—*Catherine Marshall*

94

The texture of my romantic life is
flecked with many repeated fights that
go nowhere. It's difficult to change,
but I know that a calm request will
reap more results than an argument.

The characters portrayed by Elizabeth
Taylor and Richard Burton in the movie
Who's Afraid of Virginia Woolf? Are a perfect example of a couple fighting for the
sake of the drama and the battle. Despite
the hysterics, in the end nothing changes
between them. The viewer knows that the
couple has been in the same situation in
the past and will be so again. We all need
to blow off steam once in a while, and
who better to do this with than a partner
who you know will stay around and who
is infuriating anyway? The danger is in
making this behavior a regular practice.

If you find yourself having the same
purposeless argument with your man, for

your own well-being consider putting a stop to it. Make a resolution to examine this phenomenon, and then find another person to listen to your complaints. Practice saying, "I feel . . ." before you say anything else to your man. Try to avoid a conversation that starts, "You always . . .". Concentrate on what you feel about the issue without listing his many other faults. Next, ask for the change that you would like. Make it a reasonable request. Start small for a higher possibility of success.

The basic discovery about any people is
the discovery of the relationship
between its men and women.
—Pearl S. Buck

~ 95 ~

*I argue about the same things over
and over. If I pull back from the
argument, I help myself.*

One word from the man in your life
about a certain topic, and you're off and
running. You've gotten into a pattern of
arguing with him over and over about
the same subjects—whether the topic is
your mother or his, vacations, money,
sex, or housekeeping issues. Perhaps you
feel that nobody ever wins these arguments—or that he always wins. Later,
you don't seem to remember how the
argument started and realize that nothing
has changed as a result.

When you check yourself and stop
fighting—either stop talking or leave the
situation—your mind will clear for you to
see what's going on in a way you never
could before. You'll have time to look
beneath the surface of the fights to see

what's really motivating them. Does he just need attention? Do you need more help with the kids and time alone with him to connect? Are the fights a way to finally be together? What about your family backgrounds? Use your time alone to think about these deeper causes of fighting. Get out of the fighting loop. Don't be intimated by the temporary quiet that results. A better life together is on the horizon.

People are usually more convinced by
reasons they discovered themselves
than by those found by others.
—Blaise Pascal

~ 96 ~

When I'm angry at a man, I'll try to think about psychology and the reasons why I'm angry.

Selma walks in the door and the first thing she sees are dishes in the sink and her son's uncompleted homework. She hears giggles from her husband and son as they roughhouse. It is 8:30 P.M., time for their eight-year-old to be in bed, but he isn't anywhere near being ready for sleep. Selma yells at her husband and at her son, calling them irresponsible, and says they make her sick and that she wished she never came home. They guiltily obey her orders. Her son mutters, "I don't know why you have to yell so much." Selma feels like the worst mother in the world.

How can Selma think about psychology when her anger has been aroused? How can you? But if Selma tries, at least afterwards, to assess her role in this scene, she'll remember her father yelling at the family for the same types of reasons when he came home every day. She'll connect her husband's irresponsibility with what she's heard about her father-in-law. *He's* acting just like *his* father did. *She's* duplicating *her* father's behavior.

By acknowledging this connection, Selma will gain a sense of control over her words and actions, and her husband won't be able to make her feel quite as "nuts" as he usually does. Selma will realize that the way she's been reacting isn't going to change anything and that she'll have to consider different ways of approaching the situation.

If we let our friend become cold and selfish and exacting without remonstrance, we are no true lover, no true friend.
—Harriet Beecher Stowe

~ 97 ~

*Being right in a fight won't get me
closer to a man. I will become more
sensitive to different situations
without forfeiting my opinions.*

At Jessica and Steve's Memorial Day
weekend barbecue, Steve cooked
outdoors on the grill while talking to
two male friends they'd invited. Jessica
came outside, took a look at the gas
barbecue, and started fiddling with
the knobs.

"This fire is much too hot—everything's getting dried out. What are you
doing?" she asked. "Don't touch anything," Steve said. "Well I'd better, or
there'll be nothing to eat," she replied,
picking up the fork and tongs and moving
the burgers and steaks to the side of the
grill. Steve turned red and stormed away.
Jessica had been right about the meat—
she saved the dinner from being dried

out—but she had also caused a rift in her relationship with Steve.

Needing to prove to a man that you're right is not necessarily helpful. You may think that if you're right you'll be loved, but that's not usually the case. Maybe you think you can't have an opinion unless you prove it's the right one. That's also untrue. You and your man are both entitled to your opinions, and you need to respect each other's positions, no matter how "dried out" they may seem. If Jessica had privately asked Steve to lower the grill temperature, he might have cooperated and there would have been no fight—as there was that night after the guests had left.

The only good is knowledge
and the only evil is ignorance.
—Socrates

~ 98 ~

A quiet man can be as provocative
as any loud, angry guy.
When I get angry at a quiet guy,
I won't be down on myself.

Ashley says: "Everyone tells me that my
boyfriend, Edgar, is a dream. He's so
quiet and gentle. And I do love him a
lot. I think there's something wrong
with me, though, because there are
times when I just feel like smacking
him—which is weird, because I'm not a
violent person. We both work at home.
Recently, he would walk through my
office about every half hour and cough
several times. This would distract me
but by the time I would look up he'd be
back in his office. He'd had a cold for a
few days, but he'd refused to take anything for it or call a doctor. He'd give me
a hangdog look when he coughed that
made me feel like screaming at him,

'What do you want from me?' He was trying to get me to take care of him, I guess. But why couldn't he just ask? Sometimes he'll lie down and sigh a big sigh. If I ask what's wrong, he'll say, 'Nothing.' It drives me crazy. Or if we go to a movie that I pick out, he'll look at his watch all night like he can't wait for it to end. If I ask him if he wants to leave, he'll say no. That makes me furious. What's wrong with me?"

Ashley, nothing's wrong with you. Your boyfriend is no saint. He's unconsciously angry and passive-aggressive, which means he expresses his hostility in covert, quiet ways. Tell him you'd like to know his feelings directly. Reassure him that his negative side is okay with you, and he should accept yours, too.

Resolve to be thyself; and know that
he who finds himself loses his misery.
—Matthew Arnold

~ 99 ~

*The blast of a man's rage can
freeze my personality. I will put
myself out of range and build
a wall to protect myself.*

Repeat this sentence and commit it to memory: "Beneath anyone's rage are helpless and weak feelings." Knowing this will help you to feel less scared if you are with an easily enraged type and he starts to roar. The louder he yells, the more depressed he really is and the more helpless he feels. He is not the strong man he sounds like, and he's not going to leave you because he's displeased.

There is no reason why you should erase who you are to please him. There is no reason to feel that there is anything wrong with you because this man has a bad temper. If you've studied his psychological history, you'll find that someone in his family yelled a lot. Perhaps in your family someone had a bad temper and that's why you put up with this kind of treatment.

Sally had been seeing Saul for a year. His loud voice made Sally cringe. When Saul yelled at Sally because she had dyed her hair, Sally stopped and let it become gray. Suddenly she looked old—not an asset in her work as a real estate agent in a young community. A friend and colleague made her realize that she had a right to look good for herself and her business, even if Saul felt insecure about it. Sally's gone back to dyeing her hair and calmly told Saul to back off. He did.

To have one's individuality completely
ignored is like being pushed quite
out of life. Like being blown out as
one blows out a light.
—Evelyn Scott

~ 100 ~

If I'm going to stay up all night,
I'll do it for sex—not a fight!
Endless discussions don't get me anywhere.

Let's look at Ruby and Manny.

As a stewardess, Ruby is frequently away. She's married to Manny, an executive at a food corporation who travels, too. When they're not together, they'll have four-hour phone conversations—or rather, arguments—in the middle of the night. There will be furious hang-ups, calls back to apologize, then more hang-ups. They're both exhausted the next day. Mostly, the fights are about jealousy. If Ruby's away, Manny is suspicious she's having sex with pilots, passengers— anyone. If Manny's away, Ruby's suspicious about secretaries and clients.

Ruby and Manny love each other, but they're afraid that being physically apart means death to the relationship.

So they act like some mothers do when they're away from their children—they worry and drive the kids crazy. If Ruby decides she's had enough of these all nighters, she should look into herself for the sources of her insecurity. Maybe she can help Manny feel more secure and help him to look into his background for the source of his insecurity. Couples therapy will help them reconnect in a better way, so that in the future if they stay up all night it will be for sex, not fights.

Years may wrinkle the skin, but to give up enthusiasm wrinkles the soul.
—Samuel Ullman

~ 101 ~

Violence and threats of violence cannot be allowed in my life. Either a man abides by this, or he is history.

If you stay with a man who has been violent without having set an ultimatum and sticking by it, you are putting your life in danger.

Jill met Stuart at a club one night. They danced the night away and slept together that night. After several months of bliss, Jill moved into Stuart's apartment. Soon after she moved in, they had a fight over the fact that Jill was supposed to work late every night for a month because of a project. Stuart was suspicious and thought she was seeing someone else. When Jill said she was leaving to take a walk, Stuart grabbed her and threw her on the floor, where she banged a knee and her arm. Stuart immediately calmed down and the fight was over. Two weeks later, Jill was angry at Stuart for flirting with a friend at a party. She yelled at him and he hit her across the face. Jill thought about leaving, but decided that the incident had been her fault. Anyway, she no longer had her own apartment.

Jill has to seek help with a couples therapist immediately and tell Stuart that unless he goes with her, she is leaving. She should find her own place or move in with a friend or family member. Jill needs help to feel strong enough to move out. Her life is in danger. She needs therapy or a crisis center for support. She will survive emotionally just fine without this man.

*But powerlessness is still each
woman's most critical problem. . . .
It is at the root of most of her
psychological disorders.*
—Toni Carabillo

Part 6

Enhancing Your Insight and Awareness

My pattern of loving cruel men
can change when I'm ready.
I deserve a better, gentler life.

Are love and pain connected in the heart?
Monkeys have been known to return to
an artificial surrogate "mother" even
after scientists have wired the imitation
to give off shocks intermittently when
touched. Eventually, to a monkey, or a
human, warmth and pain can become so
closely associated they can't have one
without the other. Children in families
who experience good times together followed by intense periods of emotional or
physical cruelty and suffering learn to
expect pain in a loving relationship.

Diana has been with cruel men for
years. They're all like her father, who was
a lot of fun on camping trips, treasure
hunts, and adventures, but who was also
explosive. He would hit the children

randomly when there was any trouble and berate them verbally when they didn't win at sports. Diana's current boyfriend, Jed, is the same way. After a great weekend playing tennis, camping, or cooking together, there might be a fight where he hits her and she goes home sobbing. Diana gravitates back to Jed because everything else between them is good. But she also goes back because she thinks she doesn't deserve better, that love means pain, that she's defective and no one else will want to be with her. If Diana had a different upbringing, she would not be attracted to the Jeds of the world and would meet gentler men. All she has to do is decide that she's had enough of cruelty.

If you're never scared or embarrassed
or hurt, it means you never
take any chances.
—Julia Sorel

*In the long run, being emotionally
separate can really improve romance.*

Emotional separateness, even though it
doesn't involve either of you moving
out, can cause more anxiety than actually breaking up. This separateness
means that when you are upset about
a situation and you know he won't be
helpful and might even be destructive,
you do not in any way—even through a
fight—try to get support or a reaction
from him. You reach out to others
instead. By the same token, you do not
try to discover what is bothering him
when he has a problem. And you don't
try to help him if he seems depressed or
anxious or angry. You are willing to
experience loneliness and rage and hurt
and fear and sadness—and not take any
action (unless, of course, you are in
physical danger).

Because emotional separateness can be so painful, many couples split up before they have allowed themselves to become truly separate people. When a man or woman gets to this stage, he or she may also feel so angry that they feel they have to leave. But you should wait. As truly emotionally separate people, you give each other the distance to grow and change. Although it may feel as if you have one foot out the door, stop walking. And see what happens.

*Let there be spaces in
your togetherness.*
—Kahlil Gibran

~ 104 ~

*Romance makes me fuzzy and I lose
my center. I'll hold onto my good
judgment in the midst of love.*

Be alert. When trying to establish a relationship with a man, there is the real
danger that you might give up what you
feel and want. You must resolve not to
lose your center, especially since what you
want and feel is probably better for you—
and for the relationship—in the long run.

There are many reasons why you
might lose yourself: because he's wonderful in bed; because he's so persuasive;
because anger intimidates you; because
he seems more confident and better able
to live without you than vice versa. So he
wears you down. You find yourself doing
things you don't want to—being talked
into going sailing though you get very
seasick, going to a nightclub though you
hate loud music. There are women who

are talked into "swinging sex" because they're afraid they'll lose the guy otherwise. And, of course, women are frequently coerced into sex in general by men they know. Women go along with religious and fanatic groups because they don't want to lose a man who wants them to join.

Remember that your needs come first. Reach out for support so that you hold on to your desires, your good judgment, and your inner self.

Without self-confidence we are
as babes in the cradle.
—Virginia Woolf

~ 105 ~

It's easy to complain that a man has no feelings, but I'm not always sure what my own real feelings are. Knowing what I really feel takes some work.

Stacey tells us: "I was furious at Leo, my fiancé, when he said that he couldn't set a date for the wedding because he didn't know how he felt about marriage. He had a lot of doubts about whether marriage ever works and thought that maybe we should wait. 'Why spoil a good thing?' he said. I wanted to kill him right then and there. How dare he make us postpone the wedding! Six months later he decided he could handle it. We set a date and booked a hall. The invitations went out. I suddenly came down with colitis, which the doctor said was caused by nerves. A therapist helped me see that I was deathly afraid of getting married. I guess I felt that my parents wouldn't be there for me anymore, that I'd lose them, and that Leo wouldn't come through for me. I have a lot more compassion for Leo now. It's much harder to know what I really feel than I thought."

Are you really comfortable with sadness, anxiety, disappointment, and anger, among other feelings? Do you feel confident enough to let your man know when he hurts you emotionally? Or are there certain feelings that make you feel embarrassed and ashamed? Do you secretly look down on people who are fearful or anxious? Think about this before you condemn him for being out of touch with his feelings.

We are not born all at once, but by bits. . . . Our mothers are racked with the pains of our physical birth; we ourselves suffer the longer pains of our spiritual growth.
—Mary Antin

*When I feel compelled to try and
change a man who will not change,
the reasons I act this way lie
somewhere within me.*

You're trying too hard to change him,
and he shows no sign of making a
change, but you can't stop yourself. It's
time to look at your childhood. Phoebe's
father was, and is, a destructive and nasty
man. He would call Phoebe stuck-up and
snooty for wanting to do well in school,
laugh at her if she didn't know something, and criticize her frequently. Today
at age thirty, she is with Alexander. He
can be nasty like her father, but he's rich
and is interested in art, as is Phoebe.
Each time Alexander is nasty, Phoebe lec-
tures him about treating her better. She
tries to make him understand why he
acts the way he does (because his father
abused his mother). She tells him how

angry she is. She asks him to apologize, and occasionally he does. Later, however, he'll be nasty and critical again.

Phoebe is trying to "fix" her father by trying to "fix" Alexander, who behaves in a similar way. She's trying to get Alexander to give her the love she missed as a child. She has a choice: she can give up on him and put this energy into her-self. She can find ways to get love and recognition from other sources.

Far from being the basis of the good society, the family, with its narrow privacy and tawdry secrets, is the source of all our discontents.
—Edmund Leach

~ 107 ~

The more I struggle to control a man,
the less control I have. I didn't believe
this for a long time, but I see it now.

Racquel says, "When I first met Arthur
I couldn't believe his clothes—they were
so geeky. It was like he had to show
everybody what a drab, poor background
he had come from. And he's not a drab
person at all. So I bought him clothes for
every possible occasion. He'd wear them
right away and would look fabulous.
Then I noticed that he never wore them
again. When I went to his apartment, I'd
find them stuffed in the back of his
drawers or his shelves. 'I forgot it was
there,' he'd say when I asked why he
didn't wear something. 'I just can't be
bothered,' was his explanation. I lectured
him about it, yelled at him, even cried.

"Then I got a new job and no longer
had the time for Arthur's clothing

problem. For a few months, he looked worse than ever. Then one day he showed up looking great for a party given by some people he does business with. I realized then that he knows the difference, but that he'll only make the effort to look good when he wants to. I can't force it. I feel a little freer now, but I still want to control him. When we're going someplace special to me, I'll still pick out an outfit for him to wear, and sometimes he'll wear it. I'm a work in progress on this."

When you try to control a man, you set up a power struggle you may not have expected. All you can do is tell him what you'd like. The rest is up to him.

The fullness of life is in the hazards of life . . . [we] can turn defeat into victory.
—Edith Hamilton

*When I tell myself—instead of telling
him—what to do, I have a better day.
I can let go of trying to get others
to do what I want.*

There are many reasons why you concentrate on your man instead of on
yourself. Maybe you tell him what to do
instead of telling yourself because you
don't think much of yourself, like Vicky.
She made Austin's career the focus of
her life while neglecting her own work.
Vicky had a low opinion of herself and
little respect for her own intelligence
and potential. Her parents had always
pointed to her brother as "the smart
one," so, in her mind, it was not a great
leap to think of her husband as "the
smart one" in their marriage. Vicky felt
she didn't deserve and need time for
herself because she wasn't smart
enough. Remember that your own life

and career deserve your full attention and concern.

It takes practice to stay on track and not get diverted by your man's needs and problems. As a woman, you were probably taught to put the needs of others first. But this can be changed. You can flex and strengthen those brain pathways providing positive reinforcement that lead to your own fulfillment. And you may be surprised to see that, by leaving him to his own devices, the man in your life may make changes that you had wanted him to make but had been unable to force on him. Remember that no one likes being told what to do. He won't have to plant his heels in as firmly if you've stopped telling him what to do and are telling yourself what to do instead.

I do not wish [women] to have power over men; but over themselves.
—Mary Wollstonecraft

~ 109 ~

*Aha! I just realized I reward negative
behavior with a lot of attention!
A man gets so much attention from
me by being bad, why should he
ever be good?*

"I don't want to be like the shrew in
Shakespeare," says Amy. "But when
David keeps me waiting, I just get
furious and can't stop myself." One way
for Amy to help herself is to realize that
she is being set up to be a shrew. The
most attention David ever got from his
overwrought mother was to misbehave.
He'd come home late from school, from
soccer practice, from a friend's house.
She'd yell at him every time. She didn't
know how to relate to him and rarely
spent time talking to him if they weren't
fighting. So David unconsciously seeks
the only kind of attention he's ever
received. Deep down, he assumes he

doesn't deserve any positive attention. And with Amy willingly stepping into his mother's shoes, David continues to get a lot of this negative energy.

A lot of men suffer from this "bad boy" syndrome, getting a kick out of being bad—no matter how apologetic or remorseful they may appear—because they get the attention from "mom" that they desperately need. If you stop "rewarding" the bad stuff and no longer yell, he will eventually get the message. The only behavior that gets attention is love and cooperation.

He never regarded himself as crazy.
The world was.
            —Erica Jong

~ 110 ~

*I won't take a man's silence
personally. Family and friends
are there for me to talk to.*

The silent treatment can be infuriating.
Do you get so upset that you fill the
silence with arguments and talk "at"
him? It may sound stupid to fight for this
reason, but it's not. People need human
contact. We get it by talking as well as
through touch. It may appear as if you
need contact more than he does, but
that's absolutely not true. You maintain
the contact for him by talking and
yelling, even if he acts blasé or ignores
you. The real problem, however, is that
the yelling doesn't get you anywhere. It
makes you look bad and feel worse.

Think about your family background
and why silence is so upsetting for you.
Maybe silence means there's no love. Or
in your house family members talked a

lot "at" each other, and that's what you're used to. Where else can you get the human contact you need? Make a list of family and friends, if that helps. You will be able to bear the silence with a man when you stop yelling if you contact others in your life.

Don't take his silence personally. This is his way of avoiding his feelings. When you stop talking, watch for subtle changes in him over time. They'll definitely happen. Your silence is powerful.

Loneliness is never more cruel
than when it is felt in close
propinquity with someone who
has ceased to communicate.
—Germaine Greer

111

*A man's sarcasm or mockery
does not mean I'm a fool. I'm only
foolish to take seriously anyone
who attacks like that.*

A man's sarcastic, mocking comments
carry a lot of weight when you love the
guy. These comments, however, are a
smoke screen behind which lie anger,
hurt, anxiety, jealousy, or some other
negative feeling. But the sarcasm tells
you nothing and is a useless form of
communication used by people who are
trying to hide their true feelings, which
seem too risky to express. Sarcasm and
mockery are used by insecure people.

Seth is a man who does not know
how to express his true feelings. After
Emily joined an exercise class she badly
needed because of her weight problem,
he would pantomime exaggerated exercises, making her seem ridiculous.

"You're all going to get hot fudge sundaes?" was his sarcastic response when she said she was going out with a few of the women after class. Emily felt terribly hurt and angry until she spoke to a friend. The friend pointed out that Seth was threatened by her interest in slimming down, as he himself is overweight. Never believe what your man says if he's being sarcastic. There's a serious problem beneath the surface of these empty remarks that has nothing to do with you.

Every man is a damn fool for at least
five minutes every day; wisdom
consists in not exceeding the limit.
—Elbert Hubbard

112

When I operate under blanket
assumptions and foregone conclusions,
I gyp myself and my man.
He's not a devil or a god.
I'll stay open to the moment.

Life is confusing, so to simplify things,
we lump people into categories. You and
your man both get stuck in certain roles.
It seems that to change those fixed positions would require a blast of dynamite.
Perhaps your man is always the irritable
one, the one who raises his voice at the
drop of a hat, and you cry just as easily.
Perhaps you're the one with the energy—
the organizer and doer—and he sits
around, acting tired or unenthusiastic.
But people can change. Consider these
examples:

Ari was never a sympathetic listener.
He could barely stay awake whenever
Ann tried to talk to him about a problem.

Their lack of communication made her want to leave him. Then Ann's father became deathly ill. Ari suddenly turned into an extraordinarily sympathetic mate. Ann was shocked.

Sue loved to dance, but she couldn't get Sam to join her, no matter what the occasion. One night she came late to a party and there Sam was, dancing with a friend of theirs. Sue was furious. But a friend made her see the positive side— now Sam couldn't refuse to dance by saying he was all left feet. The experience had changed the situation. Sue did get Sam to dance after that and began to see him in a new light.

It is almost as important to know what is not serious as to know what is.
—John Kenneth Galbraith

~ 113 ~

I suffer silently in a relationship,
holding onto any secret grudges,
resentments, and disappointments.
I can change if I want.

What's hidden feels safe. You remain
silent about your needs, complaints,
and angry feelings so that they can't
cause trouble. Trouble might mean your
man will be mad at you—then, you
worry, he won't love you anymore. You
will have been bad, and he might leave.
Although you may fear this will happen,
it probably won't. Yet you remain stuck
in the position of needing to appear
sweet and accepting all the time in
order to get the approval you need.
Once in a while you may blow up like
Mount Vesuvius, then it's back to
normal. Or you may let off steam by
being critical and sarcastic about little
things that are beside the point.

The first step in learning how to speak up is to understand the reasons why you are a silent sufferer. There will be roots in your past as well as causes in the present. Maybe your man's comfortable with your emotional silence. Since most men don't bring up issues, it is unlikely that he'll do anything about your silent suffering, but that doesn't mean it has to stay this way. You can make the choice to speak up, whenever you want. You have it in your power.

Anger repressed can poison a relationship as surely as the cruelest words.
—*Dr. Joyce Brothers*

114

When a man gives me the silent treatment, I think I've done something wrong. I'll remember that this is not my fault, but that he has problems communicating.

Mitchell is a portrait artist. He can be very controlling with his wife, Gina, and their two kids. His studio is separate from the house, but he insists he can hear everything that goes on there and that they must be silent or talk in whispers. They know if he's in a bad mood when he comes in at dinnertime, because if he's angry, he is silent. They tiptoe around him when he's angry, accepting his silence as their punishment for having somehow wronged him. Gina has always been apologetic with Mitchell. One evening a friend joined them for dinner, however, and afterward told Gina how shocked she was at how tightly Mitchell controlled them. Although Gina felt angry at first, she later realized that Mitchell had been taking out all his moods on his family. The kids were miserable.

The silent treatment is potent and prevents any situation from improving. Gina has to stop taking Mitchell's behavior personally and start seeing it as his peculiar problem. She can firmly tell him that this silent treatment is bad for the kids and for her. Mitchell and Gina need help. If he won't go for help with Gina, she should go alone.

Self-respect is the root of discipline;
the sense of dignity grows with the
ability to say no to oneself.
—Abraham J. Heschel

115

I can become a real caretaker and try to save a desperate man, but this is not good for either of us. It's a loving act and not selfish or callous for me to stay separate from a man's serious issues.

Rita met Frank in a casino while on vacation. All she could see were his gorgeous smile and dark good looks. He lived in the same city she did, and they saw each other every day for a month after they returned. Frank had a good job, but he had been living with his parents since his divorce. Just until he got himself together, he said. Two months after he and Rita met, he started asking her for money, which he would say was just to carry him through to his next paycheck. Rita lent him a total of three hundred dollars before she found out that he gambled—on horses, at casinos, on ball games—which was why he lived at home.

His credit was bad and he never had any money as a result. She really cared about Frank, but when he began to get pushy about getting more money from Rita, she realized he was an addict. When Frank had money he had been generous, so Rita felt awful about saying no.

Frank is the only person who can stop his gambling addiction. And he will not stop unless he feels much worse than he does right now. Rita knows she has to stay far away from him when he demands money for gambling debts. It is caring if she tells him that she will never live with him or plan a future together unless he goes for help. Saying no is the most loving thing she can do for Frank.

God, for two people to be able to live
together for the rest of their lives
is almost unnatural.
—Jane Fonda

116

*Men and others in my life turn on my
guilt switches. But only I have the key
to turn off the guilt. I can do it.*

There's something about a woman's
chemistry that causes the seeds of guilt
to grow easily. Yet the feeding of the
guilt comes from the outside. Here's
an example.

Lorinda has not been away from
Jessica, her three-year-old daughter, since
she was born. Four of her old friends
were meeting for a get-together weekend
in a nearby hotel and Lorinda impulsively
said she would go. She then told her husband Jeffrey and her mother. Her mother
said to Lorinda, "Jessica will be so upset.
What will you tell her? Can Jeffrey get
her to sleep?" Her husband was silent
when she made her announcement but
Lorinda bravely asked him to be available
that weekend. She said she would make

plans for a sitter to help out and for Jessica to see other children.

At first Jeffrey agreed. Later he wanted to know why she wasn't taking her daughter. Wouldn't the others bring their kids? No, Lorinda said, her friends wanted an all-girl talk fest with no children. By now, Lorinda had become anxious. She began to question the whole plan. She called one of her friends. The friend managed to convince Lorinda to hold to her decision. Would you like to bet on whether or not her guilt will win out over this opportunity to have a good time?

The freer that women become,
the freer men will be.
Because when you enslave
someone, you are enslaved.
—Louise Nevelson

117

*I yearn to make a man the center of
my universe, but I know that would be
a disaster for me. My universe is large.
There are many others out there who
will be good to me, too.*

Geri knew there was something wrong in
her marriage to Walter, but it was just a
vague uneasiness until she received pic-
tures in the mail of her husband having
dinner with another woman. He admitted
to the affair and broke it off, but then
went back to the other woman. He
moved in and out of the house three
times, and Geri became more and more
depressed. She waited for him to make a
decision, because she felt frozen about
seeking a divorce. Not long after Walter
moved out yet again, Bill, an old college
friend of Geri's, called her. Conversation
was easy, since he'd been through a
divorce himself. Geri agreed to have

dinner with Bill, who was flattering and fun, but afterwards she felt as depressed as ever. When her best friend called and heard how depressed Geri sounded, she yelled at her for dwelling on Walter and not paying attention to Bill, who was treating her so much better. Geri felt as if a bucket of water had been thrown at her, and she woke up. She resolved to stop dwelling on Walter.

Habits are hard to break. Geri had been used to making Walter the center of her universe and continued to do so long after he stopped being good for her. But she can change that habit.

You need only claim the events of
your life to make yourself yours . . .
you are fierce with reality.
—Florida Scott-Maxwell

Marriage makes men feel controlled,
so I need to be flexible and patient
in discussing marriage. That doesn't
mean I'll give up what I want.

You think to yourself, "He feels controlled? By me? I don't do anything to make him feel controlled. He's the one who has to have everything his way. He's the one who's controlling." And then you might add, "Am I so controlling? Is that why I can't get married? Am I really a bitch compared to other women?"

Wait a minute. You're blaming yourself, getting defensive, or blaming him for what is a preordained situation with men. Look at our society and its jokes about marriage, Rodney Dangerfield and his "take my wife" jokes. This attitude has little to do with you or him. It's just the way men have learned to think. But men also love and need women.

Because your man feels controlled doesn't make you or him bad. When you think along the lines of blame, any conversation about marriage will be impossible. Of course you're going to be angry or upset or sad if he isn't jumping at the chance to marry you according to the plans you imagined. Think about where the pressure for you to marry is coming from: are friends or parents pushing you to get married, or is it something you really want to do? Keep your eyes on what you want. Of course if your man remains steadfastly against marriage, and marriage is what you want, move on.

The majority of husbands remind me of an orangutan trying to play the violin.
—*Honoré de Balzac*

119

*Divorce leaves people feeling
vulnerable. A man's reluctance to
remarry has more to do with his
divorce than our relationship.*

A man has scars from his divorce. He sees it as a personal failure, no matter what he says—that he's actually glad his first marriage ended, or that he and his ex-wife were wrong for each other. No matter how his first marriage ended and even if he tells you that you're very different from his first wife, he is still concerned about making another mistake—because, of course, things were better with his first wife at the beginning, too. If you've been divorced, the same fears apply to you and may impede the progress of your next romance.

Victor has been separated for three years but hasn't gotten a divorce. Deep down, he's afraid that his girlfriend, Lily,

whose divorce came through a while ago,
won't stay around. They live together but
bring up marriage in a very hesitant way
because each is afraid of being hurt
again. Lily really does want to marry
Victor, but she's waiting for him to show
her he is serious by getting a divorce. She
will have to be the brave one here—take
a risk and ask for what she wants.
Women are far braver than men about
taking a stand for intimacy and marriage.
It's the only way to get what you want.

A man should never be ashamed to
own he has been in the wrong . . .
[then] he is wiser today than
he was yesterday.
—*Alexander Pope*

120

Just because a man isn't affectionate
doesn't mean I'm wrong if I am.
It's his loss if he can't open up.

Affection is when you're physical without sex. It's the hug, holding hands, the arm around your shoulder, the kiss goodnight before you go to sleep or out to work, the cuddling in front of the TV. It's the physical contact not designed to end in an orgasm. This is the part of being physical that makes some men uncomfortable, because it represents true intimacy. It says "I'm here, I like you, I want to just be with you. I'm not proving anything." There's no performance, no demands, no expectations.

Melanie's husband turns over and goes to sleep after sex and says Melanie is too needy when she wants a hug, which makes Melanie feel bad and wrong. Tina's boyfriend hates holding hands anywhere, anytime. They've had several fights about it, but Tina hasn't been able to change his mind. Affection is seen as a female, motherly activity, although it's becoming more acceptable for men to be affectionate with their children.

Of course there's nothing wrong with Melanie and Tina wanting hugs and to hold hands—they're lovely expressions of caring. But their men either feel that their masculinity is threatened by such expressions, or they are re-enacting an old control issue over being affectionate—in other words, over doing what the woman wants! What a waste.

Females are naturally libidinous.
—Aristotle

121

The flirting my man does with another woman can drive me wild. I'll remember that it's not my fault—it's his problem. I won't let any man turn me into a screaming shrew.

Your man is unconscious as to the reasons why he flirts, but you don't have to be. Insecurity can be a cause: He may be afraid you'll leave him, so he keeps you on edge. Knowing that you're jealous makes him feel wanted and secure. He could also be expressing hostility toward you in an indirect way by flirting; if you flirt with other men, this could be his way of retaliating. Or he may want to sabotage the relationship because the closeness is threatening to him. Or, he may feel controlled by all women and flirting may be his way of making sure no one has control over him. Or he could be depressed about an event in his life (the death of a parent, career problems) and flirts to make himself feel better.

These reasons have little to do with you. Think about all these possible causes and what applies to him. If you are the one flirting and getting him jealous, you should put a stop to it. Otherwise, without berating him, tell him that you feel hurt by his flirting—that although you know he doesn't mean to hurt you, it does. Ask him to pay more attention to you when he's around other women. He may get self-righteous no matter how you put it, but let it roll off your shoulders. He got the message. Talk to someone to let off steam about how much you hate him when he flirts so you don't have exhausting and pointless battles.

I have no wish for a second husband. . . .
I like to have my own way—to lie down
mistress, and get up master.
    —Susanna Moodie

~ 122 ~

*I'll slow down and recognize that a
man has a right to have needs that are
different from mine—especially if
I want him to cooperate with me.*

You want him to make a change. Let's
say you want him to work shorter hours
so that he can spend more time with
you and the kids. Or it could be something small, like getting him to agree to
replace some of the furniture he's had
since he was single, throwing out some
old clothes that you can't stand, or
picking up your mother at the airport. If
you are stubborn and argue with him if
he doesn't do what you ask, you'll find
yourself up against a wall. He doesn't
have to do what you ask; he may not
feel the same compelling need for this
project or task. He's coming from a different place. And that may be hard for
you to take.

Give him the benefit of the doubt. Let's assume he has valid reasons that he can't verbalize and that he's not just being disagreeable. You'll have to figure it out. The new furniture may represent an upscale move that makes him feel anxious. His father didn't dress well, so he may feel that clothes are unimportant. He doesn't have to like your mother; you may not like his, after all. He will sense the difference in you if you respect his opinion when you try to work out a compromise.

Of all men's miseries the bitterest is this: to know so much and to have control over nothing.
—Herodotus

123

*If a man "forgets" an event
that is important to me, it's not
a sign of lack of love.*

"If he really loved you, he would
remember that you made that presenta-
tion at work and he'd ask about it."
That's what Sandra's mother told her
about the man Sandra was dating.
Sandra's father had always doted on
Sandra's mother, remembering every
doctor's appointment and problem her
mother had at work. But he never paid
any attention to Sandra. The men whom
Sandra meets don't call every day like her
mother does or always remember to ask
her about a cold she had or how a
meeting with her boss went. Sandra acts
a little pouty with them, like they've
done her some injury. Or she'll call them
urgently if they don't call her right away.
Men don't last long in her life.

Sandra's mother is very controlling. She doesn't let anyone have much of a life separate from hers. She gave Sandra the wrong idea about men. A man's priorities may be different from yours—talking and calling a lot are not strong points with a lot of men. But that doesn't mean they don't want a relationship. If you can make room for his different method of communicating and that occasional "forgetting" is not really a big deal, your relationship will be stronger.

If you want the present to be different from the past, study the past.
—Baruch Spinoza

124

After he's been mean to me, I really want to be seduced by a grand making-up gesture like jewelry or flowers. But if I'm bought off this way, nothing will ever get better.

Maybe he's repeatedly late for dates and keeps you waiting on street corners, or comes home to dinner two hours late every night because of work. Or much worse: He flies into rages and smashes things—or physically hurts you. (Any assault, of course, requires that you take immediate action to protect yourself by putting a safe physical distance between you and him). After he's been "bad," your man will feel regret and will want to make up. He may feel anxiety that maybe he's "done it" this time and you'll leave him. So he makes it up to you with a large gesture like a gift.

Observe whether his behavior becomes a pattern, recurring more than twice. Although you may appreciate a make-up gift, in the long run gifts—and apologies—are useless to you if nothing changes. Do what you need to protect yourself from pain. If he doesn't show up for dinner, stop making it; if he's always late to the movies, make social plans with others. If he's in a bad mood every night, leave the house. Move out if he's violent. Gifts won't help. Therapy will.

Women like to sit down with trouble
as if it were knitting.
—Ellen Glasgow

~ 125 ~

*When a man is reluctant to take
a vacation with me, I'll remind
myself that this is his problem.
He has deep conflicts about being
with a woman and having fun.*

Scott's idea of a vacation is going to a
cabin with a few guys and hunting or
fly-fishing for a week. At first Charlotte
felt hurt about this, then she got angry.
Then she got even and went away with
friends when Scott went away—but she
still felt confused and upset. Scott's
problem, however, is pretty clear. His
parents never took a vacation; his father
went hunting and made fun of neigh-
bors who "got taken in by all that
babble about travel." Scott has a sister
who took vacations until she had a
couple of bad accidents—a car wreck
and a broken leg from skiing. Now she
stays home, too.

Scott's anxiety about taking a vacation with a woman for pure fun and relaxation is very high, but it is deeply buried. Instead of confronting it, he'll put Charlotte down for wanting to take a trip. Once, he even got "sick" just before they were to leave for a long weekend with friends in the country.

Remember a time you were anxious about trying something new. This is what he feels about having fun and spending money on a vacation. Be supportive but confident about what you know would be good for your relationship—a great vacation that you both deserve.

To be reborn is a constantly recurring human need.
—Henry Hewes

~ 126 ~

*I don't want to pay the price of having
a man take control of me. Having him
care about me is good enough.*

Marvin seemed kind when Louise first
met him. He complimented Louise on
how she looked and called every day. But
then he insisted she shop only at clothing
stores he like, and was annoyed if she
didn't buy what he picked out. He was
suspicious if she was out when he called.

You want your man to care *about*
you, but if you hope that he will also take
care *of* you, expect to pay a price. He may
become so controlling that you won't be
able to pick out your own clothes each
day, like Marvin. Or you will have to take
care of him, too, and since women usually overdo in this department, you won't
get back what you put in. If you put
yourself in charge of what he eats, what
he wears, whether he exercises and with

whom, there will be no time left for you. The more he treats you as if you are his child, the greater the transference feelings will be, which means the more he'll seem like your parent to you.

Find someone who will care about you and love you—not control you.

I want the freedom to carve and chisel my own face, to staunch the bleeding with ashes, to fashion my own gods out of my entrails.
—Gloria Anzaldua

Part 7

Taking Care
of Yourself

Today I will take an emotional risk and do it differently. If I usually yell, today I'll clam up when he is upsetting. If I'm usually silent, I will speak up about my needs.

Gloria never meant to rant and rave about Jim's sloppiness. It just happened every time she noticed his clothes strewn about the house. Which was every day.

It is easy to get stuck in a rut, yelling and arguing too often, especially when you don't get what you want and need. If this is happening, it's time to try something different. Gloria finally realized that screaming had never changed anything. She waited for a quiet moment, then talked to Jim calmly about hiring a housekeeper. It took awhile, but Jim eventually agreed. Now he even picks up after himself occasionally.

You can also get stuck in the rut of being quiet and passive, like Cindy.

About once a week, Larry would stay out late without an explanation and Cindy never questioned it. Then it became four nights a week. Still, Cindy said nothing rather than start a fight. After a few months of this, she found out through a neighbor that Larry was having an affair. She cried to herself but still could not confront him. Larry eventually left. Don't expect anyone to stick up for you if you don't stick up for yourself.

The strongest principle of growth
lies in human choice.
—*George Eliot*

~ 128 ~

*Taking risks for what I want with
a man is hard, but I have the courage
to do it. I am proud of myself
for taking a risk.*

Risk-taking requires courage—but you've
got it. He may withdraw his love for a
while. He may give you the silent treatment. All because you took a risk for
what you believe in. Maybe you went
back to school and he doesn't like that.
Or you let him know how upset you are
because he doesn't discipline the children. Or you finally told him you don't
like the way he screams and curses when
he's angry—and you walk out when he
gets that way. Every step you take
requires just as much courage as if you
went into outer space or into a war zone.
You won't get a Purple Heart or a presi-
dential audience for what you do, but
you'll deserve it just the same.

If taking such a risk has the potential to put you in physical danger with your man, you must seek help before taking any major steps. You must always make your physical safety a priority.

The risks you take will be, for the most part, hidden and unrewarded by society, as many of a woman's accomplishments are. Supportive people in your life will appreciate what you're trying to do, but it will be the pride in yourself that will mean the most, and you will carry that with you always.

Avoiding danger is no safer in the long run . . . Life is either a daring adventure or nothing.
—Helen Keller

~ 129 ~

*I can give up the myth of Prince
Charming; no men are perfect.
But I can take emotional risks
to get what I want.*

When you love a man and want to be
with him, it feels risky to tell him what
he doesn't want to hear. It feels risky to
do something he doesn't want you to do.
But unless you are true to yourself, your
life will be a patchwork of lost wishes,
hopes, and ambitions—a nightmare
instead of a dream come true.

Susan risked everything. She was
scared to tell Sean, whom she lived with,
that she wanted a child. Their joint
silence about the subject made her
nervous. Expecting the worst, she told
him what she wanted some day. He was
shocked and horrified. He said she was
not the mothering type. Susan was distraught but did not back down, even

when he threatened to end the relationship if she had a child. They argued for weeks. Susan decided to leave, a difficult decision at the age of 36, and started to look for her own place. Finally, as she was due to sign a lease, Sean softened. He said that childraising might be right for him after all and agreed to have a child with her. Susan had taken a risk, stayed strong despite Sean's opposition, and ended up getting the life she wanted. You can, too.

I have a woman's fears, but they cannot make me into a hypocrite or a slave.
—Madame de Staël

~ 130 ~

Thinking of a lover as a close friend doesn't always work. I'll look to others for the support of my inner yearnings and true self.

He's great in bed, he loves you enough to make a commitment, and you both like to dance and play tennis—but he spaces out when you talk about problems at work or when you're upset with your mother. He turns on a football game when you talk about your feelings. Often men seem to have a gene missing when it comes to emotional nurturance. So giving up or cutting yourself off from a support network of friends just because there's a man in your life can be dangerous.

Let's say you yearn to write short stories. You start one and show it to him and he either says nothing or tells you it's terrible. So you put it away and never write again. This is the same as amputating an arm because he things it is flabby. Your man has a whole slew of problems and emotional issues—some of which he takes out on you just because you're with him. Yet women change their lives because of just one man's opinion—when the opinion may be as useless or irrelevant as a five-year-old's advice. No matter how wonderful he may appear, keep your dear friends near.

Give me one friend, just one, who meets
the needs of all my varying moods.
—Esther M. Clark

131

I won't look to just one man to quell the depressed and lonely feelings. There is a whole world of people out there.

Feelings of emptiness and loneliness are part of the human condition, and these feelings can be the result of a childhood where no one responded to you and your inner emotional needs. The places in yourself that feel empty should not cause you shame. They exist in all of us. Once you allow yourself to know where your emotional voids are, you can take constructive action to fill those spaces with good friends and activities that give you pleasure. It can be destructive to pretend that the voids don't exist.

Carla often felt lonely and scared. But from an early age, she had always had a boyfriend who would do anything she asked. As long as the guy was adoring—and Carla was beautiful and easily adored—she felt fine. When the guy left, she crashed. There always seemed to be another guy around to take his place, however, so she never really had to deal with her underlying depression, a result of a childhood with an explosive and violent mother and an alcoholic and passive father. As Carla got older, she became frustrated at her inability to establish a long-term relationship. After a friend pointed out to Carla that she was overly demanding of a man's time and attention, she sought help. Carla became aware of, and was able to deal with, the inner loneliness she had been denying. Because she was able to heal, her next relationship became the permanent one she had wanted.

What a lovely surprise to discover how un-lonely being alone can be.
—Ellen Burstyn

132

*I make up excuses to myself as to
why I don't ask for what I need.
What I need is important—
no more excuses!*

Courage and confidence are the two
important ingredients for being successful when you want a relationship.
And you need both when you are the one
to say you'd like a commitment. He may
say, "I don't love you enough," "We don't
have that kind of relationship," or "Are
you nuts? No woman can tie me down. I
guess we better slow this down." And
then it's over. These are harsh words to
risk hearing from someone you care
about, which is why you need courage to
bring up the topic. (Of course *only* bring
up making a commitment if you've been
seeing each other regularly for several
months and your intuition tells you it's
the right time.)

Maybe a good friend will tell you that you have guts for asking him to be monogamous. But more likely, your courage will go unacknowledged. Like much else in life, if you don't give yourself credit for this, no one else will. You're the backstage crew of romance, doing the work that gets the show on the road. Aren't you amazing?

You took the world's soul,
Thrilled it by your daring,
Lifted the uncaring
And made them joyous men.
—Angela Morgan

133

*I won't wait for a man to appreciate me
before I feel good about what I've done.*

How easy it is to be taken for granted by
your mate. You work so hard and make
managing everything look effortless, yet
your man never seems to notice. You can
easily get stuck feeling resentful—or just
fail to recognize that you deserve applause
for what you do. Women's work, as we all
know, is usually undervalued or devalued.

Monica told Fred that she needed
to hear a "thank you" when she planned
a vacation for them, or hear him say,
"great dinner" when she cooked. Fred
argued about this, saying he felt controlled, and at best would only tell her a
half-hearted "thank you." Monica praised
herself, but she didn't feel better. She
felt incredibly sad.

Then she realized her opinion had
not mattered much at home while she

was growing up—that her parents had rarely praised her for anything. Monica recognized that she had been in the habit of thinking her opinions were unimportant. Suddenly she felt stronger. She began to post notes to herself with encouraging phrases, got support from friends, talked to herself about what a great person she was, and ignored Fred. She stopped doing as much for him—if he wasn't appreciative of her efforts, why should she work so hard? Fred got the message and became more appreciative, though Monica no longer feels that his compliments are as essential to make her feel good.

Housework is what woman does that nobody notices unless she hasn't done it.
—Evan Esar

~ 134 ~

*I'm confident enough and brave
enough to ask a man to put his love
for me into words.*

He's not Romeo, but you know he's com-
mitted. Now is the time to bring in the
words of love you need. Maybe you've
been together so long you've stopped
saying "I love you." It's time to start it
up again. As you know, you don't get
anything for nothing. There is a risk,
however, in asking for compliments and
words of love.

Valerie's boyfriend pats her on the
head when she tells him she loves him.
She wants to scream, "I'm not a pet—talk
to me!" She decided to tell him what she
needs. One night when they were having
a romantic dinner she said, "I love you
and I know you feel the same way. But I
need to hear you say it." Her boyfriend
laughed and said, "Of course I love you,

silly." Which was good enough for Valerie. When she got dressed up for his office party, she felt confident enough to ask him to tell her she looked nice. He said what she needed to hear.

You show strength when you ask for what you need in such a direct way. Remember that this is a good move, a brave step to take for the more romantic relationship that you deserve. But only take it if the odds are good that he'll respond well.

We can only learn to love by loving.
—Iris Murdoch

～ 135 ～

I don't know how much I want to compromise with regard to what I want from a man. But I do know that I'm the only one who should decide that and not let others tell me what to do.

A relationship is surely about compromise. You may ask, "How much compromise do I have to agree to? When do I decide that enough is enough and look for someone else or enjoy being alone for a change?"

When you're undecided about a relationship, you may speak to a lot of people. You might even become obsessed by your indecision and talk about your relationship all the time. As a result, you may get a lot of input from friends and family. Some people may tell you to break up with your man and they may be incensed that you're putting up with his behavior another minute! Others may be more reflective about your relationship and support whatever decision you might choose to make.

Keep in mind that people speak from whatever place they're in, in their own life. No one can or should make a decision for you. For example, Hannah loves Martin but Martin can only tolerate about six months of togetherness. Then he's gone again. They've broken up and gotten back together again five times. She loves him more than any man she's met, so the decision to continue seeing him or not is a difficult one. As much as your family and friends want to help, and may be right in what they say, only you know what you need. But don't compromise out of fear. The fear will pass once you make the change.

Forgiving is not forgetting,
it's letting go of the hurt.
—Mary McLeod Bethune

136

I will follow the advice of twelve-step programs and say, "I'll keep a loving blanket of detachment around me in the face of his problems. That is better for both of us."

Imagine that you come to a raging stream you need to cross. You could walk through it and get soaked—and possibly hurt—or you could cross a log bridge that spans the river, staying out of harm's way. You have a choice about how to get to the other side. In the same way, you can choose whether to plunge into your man's problems—and get hurt—or keep out of them.

Penny's guy, Wade, is a computer salesman and a nervous type. Penny is an art dealer at a gallery. They took an apartment together where the rent was high, so they really needed both incomes. At the time, Wade was having problems dealing with his office politics and would call Penny frantically every day at work for advice. Penny was a wreck—worrying that Wade would quit his job and they'd lose their apartment. She would talk to him a long while each day to try to calm him down, but his calls became an intrusion at her job. Wade also kept her up at night with his need to talk about work. Penny worried that the distractions of Wade's job problems and her lost sleep were jeopardizing her job. She loves Wade but decided she couldn't fix his life. She told him he needed to get help with his career problems and that she would listen briefly to his problems once a day but not offer advice. She also gave him some names of therapists who help with career problems. Penny is being detached but also loving and caring. The limits she sets will be best for them both in the end.

Love does not consist in gazing at each other, but in looking outward together in the same direction.
—Antoine de Saint-Exupéry

137

*It's not worth it to get sick over a guy.
I will take care of my health and allow
my feelings to come out so I don't have
to use sickness to express myself.*

Sometimes you get a headache or feel
dizzy because you're nervous. This is a
form of *somatizing,* or expressing feelings
through illness. It's easy to forget about
your health when you're upset about a
man. It's easy to stop exercising or eat
the wrong food because you're
depressed. It's scary, but important for
you to know, that studies have shown
that there is a link between the onset of
terrible illnesses, like cancer, and the loss
of a loved one through divorce or death.

So what's more important—your life
or his? Aren't you worth something, even
if he's not around? How will you be
ready for the next good thing that happens in your life if you're ill? When

Samantha found out that Nicholas had had an affair with another woman, she took to her bed for days. Awful pains in her back made even walking torture. Although she had been a marathon runner, she was barely able to hobble about—even though x-rays showed that nothing was really wrong. Finally, a close friend read her the riot act. "You're destroying your life for that creep instead of thinking of ways to get back at him—instead of letting him have it with your feelings," she said. Samantha finally got furious—and got out of bed. The pain lessened, and soon she was physically back to her old self.

The sorrow which has no vent in tears may make other organs weep.
—Henry Maudsley

138

Just because a man sounds intelligent
doesn't mean he should be allowed
to criticize me. I don't have to
take his criticisms.

Criticism can be subtle when your man never actually says he's angry and his comments even sound intelligent. He's still being critical. Here's an example.

Eric is a psychologist. Rachel never wins a fight with Eric because he analyzes her. He'll say, "Look Rachel, you don't want to help me take care of the apartment because of your mother. She was a neat freak and you're rebelling against her. Take out your anger on her, not on me." Or, "You have trouble listening when I talk. You interrupt a lot and that's because no one in your family listens to anyone else. I'm saying this for your own good." He'll say these things with a smile, but they make Rachel feel awful and confused. She feels as if she cannot respond.

As a child, Rachel had often been criticized by her mother, so she doesn't recognize that she should be treated differently. Eric's analysis of Rachel is really just a sneaky form of criticism. Eric is actually a very angry guy. Rachel needs to put a stop to what Eric is doing and insist that he express what he really feels and wants. Eric can say, "I'm angry because the apartment is a mess. We need to do some cleaning. Let's make a schedule." When Eric talks without the criticism, Rachel will readily do the work and won't feel awful.

No one can make you feel inferior
without your consent.
—*Eleanor Roosevelt*

139

A man may seem tougher than I am, but the strong side of me is just hidden. I can uncover and draw upon my strength.

The popularity of movies and TV shows about mobsters in therapy (e.g., *Analyze This, The Sopranos*) attests to the fact that we are fascinated by the idea that a tough guy's inner core may be filled with anxieties, insecurities, or loneliness. Although you may be in a relationship with someone who seems to be a "tough guy," it is important to remember that you have your own inner strength—and that he has a vulnerable and emotional side.

Juanita is supposedly the jealous one in her marriage. Carlos is friendly with everyone, including women. Wherever they go, he always ends up going off somewhere and talking for hours with an attractive woman. Juanita feels like his mother—looking for him and telling him it's time to leave. Carlos only laughs when she talks about feeling jealous and left out. He says she makes too much out of nothing. Juanita knows, however, that Carlos would feel the same way in her position. In fact, when they went to an art gallery opening, and Juanita talked with a man there for the entire evening, Carlos was the one to say, "Let's go." When he interrogated her about the man at the gallery, Juanita let Carlos know that he was just as jealous as she was.

Just because your man may seem tough doesn't mean that you don't have the same toughness in you. By the same token, he can also feel vulnerable and under the right circumstances will cry and show his fragile side.

I believe that men are generally still a little afraid of the dark, though the witches are all hung, and Christianity and candles have been introduced.
—Henry David Thoreau

~ 140 ~

The practice I've had dealing with a
difficult romantic relationship has
been worthwhile. Today, if my
father or boss gives me trouble,
I won't take it personally. I'll
know what action to take for myself.

Carla was a legal secretary when she met her husband, Don, a lawyer at the office. Outside the office, Don would question Carla as if she were a witness and would make negative comments about her. She wondered if this was her fault until she noticed that her husband also acted that way around other people in the office. She came to the conclusion that his behavior was his problem. Carla went back to law school herself and through this experience gained self-confidence. She became better at stopping Don when he started with his grilling techniques. Her risks paid off: Don now tries to control his bad habit of putting others down. This experience also proved useful when Carla interned in an office where her boss was as critical as Don had been. With the same confidence, and polite firmness she had used with Don, Carla managed to get her boss to treat her with respect.

You're working on your own personality and confidence when you deal with a difficult man. You can become more confident and secure as you learn to separate a difficult man's issues from your own. The security you gain will help you deal with the next difficult man you encounter, whether it be your boss, your father, or a friend.

I've learned silence from the talkative;
tolerance from the intolerant, and
kindness from the unkind. I should not
be ungrateful to those teachers.
—Kahlil Gibran

141

Sexy bad guys attract me, but their problems cause me grief. I need to set firm limits to protect myself.

Men who act out are often attractive to women—they're the bad boys, they're "cool." They're also losers in many ways. A guy who races his car on the highway can end up dead. If a man cuts out of work to have a good time, he can end up getting fired. Anyone who drinks too much, uses illegal drugs, or gets into physical fights is trouble. These men can be very passionate and sensitive, which makes them attractive. But there are plenty of passionate men who don't have these problems.

    John is very athletic and muscular. His square jaw, dark hair, and charming smile captivated Diane right away. But after dating and lending John money for a year, Diane found out that he was gambling on football games and races. She stopped lending him money. Soon after, he wanted her to give up her apartment and move in with him. Although Diane loved John, she refused. She was sure John would be out of a job and an income very soon, he argued with his boss so much, and she didn't want to be in the position of supporting him. Diane had done the right thing: she protected herself.

*You've got to love what's
lovable, and hate what's hateable.
It takes brains to see the difference.*
—Robert Frost

142

There's a long list of what men haven't done for me. But today I will ask my man for what I need without mentioning past wrongdoings.

Clearing the slate is a liberating experience, but can be so hard to do because of the ways your man has hurt or neglected you in the past. Perhaps he has embarrassed you in front of your friends more than once or has forgotten more of your anniversaries than he has remembered. Maybe he doesn't do enough for you in bed or never picks up around the house. Or maybe he hasn't made a meal in ages or can't seem to listen to you talk about a problem for more than two minutes. There may be many conflicts, but is it possible you can let them go today?

Try talking to him in a direct, calm, manner that will allow both of you to really communicate. Perhaps you say that you've tried this already. But be truthful: Did the conversation quickly turn into an argument? After a ten-second silence did you lace into him with, "I knew you wouldn't . . ."? Or did you ask for what you wanted very meekly, as if you weren't entitled—as if you were a child? Or perhaps you rushed through the points you wanted to make without giving him time to mull it over? When you believe that what you want is right, and you also know that his problems prevent him from giving, you communicate with him in a different way. If he still refuses to give you what you want, is insulting, or doesn't want to discuss the matter, you know enough to drop it. If you say absolutely nothing in response and just wait, he will eventually realize that he has been left alone with his own smallness.

But love is blind and lovers cannot see
The pretty follies that themselves commit.
—*William Shakespeare*

～ 143 ～

*Financial support comes with strings
attached. I will not pay too high
a price to have a man support me.*

Although more women support themselves now than ever before, many women still rely on a man to support them—either because they have to or because they want to. Margaret is paying too high a price for financial security. Lee persuaded her to move in with him, then convinced her to quit her job as an accountant so that she could help him out with the books for his music company. Lee turned out to be irrationally jealous, however. He'll accuse Margaret of being involved with any man they encounter. In a frenzy, he'll pack her clothes and put her bags by the door. He'll order her to leave. This behavior terrifies Margaret, in part because she has given up her apartment and has nowhere to go and in part because she's grown so dependent on Lee. Eventually, he calms down and they unpack the bags—until it starts all over again. Although Margaret is angry at times about the way Lee treats her, she mostly feels fearful of what he'll do in his next fit of jealousy.

Since she's been with Lee, Margaret has regressed from being a competent accountant earning a good income to being a scared child. She needs a support group to help her get back to who she really is.

When I die, my epitaph should read:
She Paid the Bills.
That is the story of my private life.
—Gloria Swanson

~ 144 ~

*Men don't live up to my fantasies,
especially where birthdays are
concerned, but I can create a situation
with a man that will give me good
feelings about myself.*

Tamara was crushed when her birthday
arrived and Lawrence walked in the door
with nothing. He sometimes came home
with flowers for no reason, and he loved
romantic dinners. So what was his
excuse? "I forgot, I guess. But I didn't
know you went in for that kind of thing,"
he said unapologetically. He made it
sound like a bad thing to want attention
and a gift on her birthday. It took days
for Tamara to come out of her depression
and stop feeling angry at Lawrence.

Tamara could spend hours arguing
with Lawrence to get him to see why
birthdays are important, but he just
wouldn't get it. Give up the idea of

getting your man to see the situation the same way you do, and instead ask him to go along with what you need: a present (give him an exact list with store locations), flowers, or a night out (tell him where you want to go) on your birthday. He may complain or say it feels artificial; you can be understanding but don't back down. If you feel hurt and angry that you have to go to such lengths for a birthday present, share your feelings with anyone who will be sympathetic to them—just not him. Include other friends who like to celebrate with you.

The gods approve
The depth, and not the tumult, of the soul.
—William Wordsworth

~ 145 ~

*The fantasy of breaking up with this
man can give me strength. In my
fantasy I know I'll survive and can
be happy with a different man.*

A fantasy can be like a shot of vitamin
B_{12} in that it gives you energy. It can also
give you hope. Positive imagery is frequently used by athletes. Picture your life
as a racecourse, and imagine how you'll
handle any obstacles in your path—or
hardships life brings—in a positive way.
Picture yourself surviving them all and
coming out on the other end as a wiser
person who meets men who are sexier,
who treat you better, who express their
feelings, and who are supportive. Imag-
ining makes it all seem more possible.

Sharon's breakthrough with Mike
came when she was able to fantasize
about being away from his neglect. She
felt freer, lighter, and relieved to think

that there was more to life than sitting at home and waiting for him (most days he worked until midnight). She went back to taking dance classes and even joined a dance team that performed at community events. She had a great time and met a new man. Suddenly, Mike cut back on his hours and became very attentive. Sharon had two attentive men now—a fantasy of a better life had been the first step to making it all happen.

One can never consent to creep when
one feels an impulse to soar.
—Helen Keller

~ 146 ~

*No man's love is worth sacrificing
my physical safety.*

Keisha knew Adam was an avid skier and told him that she would agree to go to a ski resort in Colorado for their honeymoon—even though she herself didn't ski. Keisha figured that she could sit at the spa or maybe try a beginning class, but that was it; she was scared to ski. When they got to the resort, however, Adam kept trying to convince Keisha to ski, telling her how romantic it would be for the two of them to go to the top of the mountain together. Adam ignored Keisha's fears, took her out of her beginner class, and insisted that she go with him to an intermediate slope. Keisha wanted to please Adam; she was thrilled to be married to him, he was so attractive and bright and personable. She figured that he knew more about the sport than she did and that he wouldn't tell her to do anything unsafe. When they got off the chair lift and Keisha stared at the steep slope, she was terrified. "You'll be fine," Adam told her, "come on," and off he went. Keisha followed, but was unable to control her speed and ended up falling and breaking her left leg.

The moral of the story is simple: You are the only one who can and should decide what is safe for you. It is very dangerous to give any man the power of a wise father figure, hoping he'll love you if you do what he says. Boys have been goading each other into dangerous activities with cries of "chicken" for years. Your judgment about what is right for you is much better than his—always.

There is a time to keep silence
and a time to speak.
—Ecclesiastes

Part 8

Staying on Your Positive, Romantic Path

147

I've given up goals because a man seemed unhappy or angry. I won't sacrifice my own hard-earned happiness any longer.

We're not all saints, and we aren't always thrilled by another's happiness. Men often become miserable when their woman "finds" herself. There are three kinds of reactions that an insecure man might have when his woman suddenly changes and is out in the world making herself fulfilled and happy in a new way. He might just sit at home and pout. He might try to compete with her in the field she is interested in. Most destructive to a relationship, however, is when a man acts out his insecurities over his woman's new-found happiness by having an affair. These types may even see a new baby in the family as a threat.

Don't blame yourself for any reaction your man may have. You can be sympathetic to his feelings of insecurity and keep the lines of communication open about how he feels about the changes that are happening. That may prevent any acting out on his part, but never blame yourself if he acts in a destructive way.

To love oneself is the beginning
of a lifelong romance.
—Oscar Wilde

148

I can keep getting more confident,
more self-aware, and psychologically
smarter even though I'm with
a difficult man. The time
has not been wasted.

Even if a man doesn't change, if you are
determined to know psychologically
what's happening between the two of
you, if you are allowing yourself to
become aware of your own behavior and
feelings, and if you are complimenting
yourself on the effort you have put into
the relationship, your confidence will
grow. Staying with him can never be
wasted time for you, even if you eventually leave your difficult man, because in
the process you will have changed from a
shrinking violet to a blooming rose.

You want to keep heading in a for-
ward direction and working on the issues.
Do not travel backward emotionally

when you stay with a difficult man.
Always put your emotional health first.
On a day-to-day basis, it may be difficult
to assess how much progress you've
made. Some days may be awful: your
confidence seems gone, you hate him and
yourself. Those days by themselves don't
count. To get a real view of what's happening, compare where you are now to
where you were last year. Do this comparison in a happy or neutral moment.
Your mental graph should be like a good
mutual fund—some downhill slides but,
overall, the trend is upward. If not, get
some help.

By annihilating desires you
annihilate the mind.
—Claude Adrien Helvetius

149

*Today I will begin to ask for the triple
A's: Appreciation, Admiration,
and Affection. I'm worth it!*

Alec grew up on a farm with five siblings.
They all worked hard from sunup to sun-
down. His parents worked hard, too, and
had little time for the kids. There was
intense competition among Alec's
brothers and sisters for any extra attention. The only warmth Alec's father had
ever shown to Alec was after he had
gotten really angry. Then his father
would feel guilty and make an effort to
be nice to Alec for a while.

Alec left the farm for the city. He
met Jeanette at a bar. Jeanette was taken
by Alec's blond, outdoorsy good looks
and they got along well, both having a
similar sense of humor. But after six
months Jeanette realized that Alec never
complimented her, whether it was for a

job promotion she received, new dress she wore, or the dinner she had given for his birthday.

Fortunately, Jeanette asked enough questions to be able to figure out that Alec was ignorant of how to express the three A's—and that he was scared to admire or appreciate, because he thought he might get hurt or lose out. Since Jeanette loved so much about Alec, she made the effort to tell him what she needed when she needed it, and he responded. She praised Alec and reassured him that her love for him was strong.

If I am not for myself, then who will be for me? . . . And if not now, when?
—Rabbi Hillel

150

*The Kodak holiday picture and the real
one are rarely the same. I'll try to stay
realistic and flexible about holidays
and to enjoy whatever happens.*

There's a lot of pressure to make a big deal
about a holiday: to have it be the best ever,
to have it live up to the Hallmark image.
Holidays are rarely perfect, however. To
begin with, you and your man may disagree about where to spend the holiday.
Spending it with one another's family can
be stressful and uncomfortable—not a
winning combination. It is important to
keep in mind that a sense of humor about
any holiday will be your best bet for getting through the rough spots. Also, neither
of you should be expected to try to live up
to anyone else's image.

In Beth's situation, her open mind
really helped. "When Elliot called at four in
the afternoon on New Year's Eve to say he

had to work late, I thought I'd kill him. We had reservations at an expensive restaurant with friends and he knew he wouldn't be able to get there until late. But I've been working on detaching and living in the moment, so I got dressed anyway and met our friends. I had a really great time. Everyone was extra nice to 'poor me.' Elliot showed up just before midnight. I felt bad for him that he'd had to work, and he seemed grateful that I wasn't mad. We were especially loving toward each other. It turned out to be one of our closest New Year's Eves."

No mockery in the world ever sounds to me as hollow as that of being told to cultivate happiness . . . . Happiness is not a potato, to be planted in mould and tilled with manure.
—Charlotte Brontë

151

*It's hard to live in the present with
wisdom gained from the past and not
hold grudges. This is a difficult goal
to strive for, and I'm proud that
I'm making the effort.*

Remembering what caused the problems
of the past is difficult because of the
painful feelings you associate with the
memories. Consider Hillary's situation.

Hillary does not learn from the past.
She loves her boyfriend, Stefan, but he's
not sympathetic. Last week she came
home distraught about her boss's harsh
criticisms. She cried on Stefan's shoulder.
He then blamed her for causing the problems at work and defended her boss.
Hillary was shocked, hurt, and furious;
she threw a glass at him and stormed out
of the house. But she should have known
this would happen. It's happened before—
in fact, it's happened every time she's

cried in front of Stefan. Hillary keeps "forgetting" what Stefan is like, so she never learns from these experiences. By now she should know enough to call a friend for comforting instead of calling on Stefan.

We're all like Hillary to some extent. It's not easy to keep your man's faults in mind, yet still enjoy him when he's sweet. It will help both you and your relationship in the long run, however, if you make a conscious effort to do so. Pat yourself on the back for trying.

Women and elephants never forget.
—Dorothy Parker

~ 152 ~

*Self-righteous critiques cover up my
real feelings of anger. I'll begin to
observe what's happening at the
moment I start criticizing.*

Mary says: "Neil always promises to fix
whatever is broken around here, but he
never gets around to it. I always have to do
it—I'm better at it, and he's so lazy. Neil
said he would try for a promotion at work,
he never even applied for the position.
He's a wimp and I yell at him, but nothing
ever changes. What do I do now?"

Remember the schoolteacher who
yelled so often that nobody listened after
a while? Yelling only works as a rare
occurrence. Otherwise, you're not taken
seriously and you just become exhausted
from your efforts. Yet each time your
man does something infuriating it's as if
your anger meter gets switched on. Start
observing what exactly is activating that

switch. Do this without blaming yourself, or the observation method will not work. No blame, remember. Keep watching yourself without trying to stop yelling at him. Just think about stopping. If you get to the point where you can tell when the anger is starting, go make a phone call to a friend or therapist. Mouthing off about him to them will help a lot.

My mother used to say, "He who angers you, conquers you!" But my mother was a saint.
—Elizabeth Kenny

*When I stop putting out other people's
fires, I have time for myself. I'll keep
this in mind, one day at a time.*

Zachary is a talented film editor; but he
can also be trouble. Edie is a lawyer.
From the beginning, Edie made a habit
of saving Zachary from the trouble he'd
created. It always came from Zack's
driving: he would run red lights, make
illegal turns, get scores of parking tickets,
be pulled over for speeding. Edie
defended him in court each time and
kept managing to get the judge to let him
keep his license. Her help was backfiring,
though. The more she did for him, the
less appreciative Zachary was. He took
her help for granted and became annoyed
if she couldn't make his court date
because of her job—which she jeopard-
ized by so much rearranging of her
schedule. Zack thought rules were

ridiculous and always denied he'd done anything wrong.

A friend finally lectured Edie on what *enabling* means: that her do-gooding was enabling Zack to continue to be a kid and that he'd only take responsibility if he hit rock bottom. Edie understood this time. She stopped defending him in court. Zack lost his license. He was then caught driving without it and was sentenced to thirty days in jail. Edie didn't even help Zack meet bail. When he got out of jail, he was a different guy. The driving problems stopped forever.

The only real answer to frustration is to concern myself with the drawing forth of what is uniquely me. This gives me the impulse and the courage to act constructively on the outside.
—Robert K. Greenleaf

~ 154 ~

Instead of thinking about men,
I'm going to spend time and
energy on myself.

From the beginning, young girls spend too much time thinking about boys—more time than they spend thinking about themselves. They wonder how to attract boys, what boys like, what they think; whether they'll see a boy at a certain place; whether a boy they like will like them back. Girls even study up on the subjects that interest the boys they like, thereby giving away large quantities of their mental energy. As a woman, you've outgrown the adolescent fixation on boys, but the problems, needs, and wants of the man in your life may still absorb too much of your time and energy. The first step out of this bad habit is to be aware that you are thinking about him more than is good for you.

The next step is to understand the fears of being abandoned or being "wrong" that push you to think about him. Greta told me, "If I don't give him all my attention and help him out, he'll find someone else and I'll be left alone." Do you really want someone who would leave you because you no longer gave him your undivided attention? Strong men will find you sexy because a truly sexy woman is one who finds herself exciting and worth her own time.

One hour of life, crowded to the full with glorious action, and filled with noble risks, is worth whole years of those mean observances of paltry decorum.
—Sir Walter Scott

Like a moth to the flame, I've been drawn to the nightmarish drama that a man has created between us. I'm strong enough to stay away from the heat.

There are men who need to argue and to create conflict where there need not be any. They may create a situation so infuriating that a woman is provoked into being the first one to yell, making the man look blameless. Celine, for example, was never one to raise her voice until she married Andy. Instead of picking up their son, Andy would forget and play ball with friends. He would also forget their anniversary and to pay bills. He could get outright nasty to waiters in restaurants. Celine would intervene and would find herself arguing with him when she didn't want to fight. Their son suffered as a result of their frequent battles.

Sometimes it feels as if you have no choice but to argue. Fights happen so fast, and you may find yourself deep into it before you realize what's happened. Think about why you need the fight. What will happen if you say nothing? The situation doesn't really improve because you fight. Know the psychological score: Are you angry at your family, as well? This may be the reason why his provocative behavior can catapult you so fast into an argument that you really don't want. Celine realized this and stopped fighting with Andy in front of their son. She regained control of herself and of the situation.

Experience is not what happens
to a man; it is what a man does
with what happens to him.
—Aldous Huxley

~ 156 ~

One man can't fulfill all my dreams.
There is so much more to life.
I won't shut myself off.

Based on medical statistics, you're probably going to outlive any man you're with. Isn't that reason enough to keep an active life going on your own? This doesn't mean having a flock of other men waiting on standby. It means keeping in touch with friends and having work that you enjoy and that sustains you. It means allowing your interests and even your dreams to exist separate from his. Some will overlap, of course, but keep an open mind. Say you both like to play golf but you've only been playing with him. Why not put together your own golf game with other women?

Among women who have lost their spouses, the ones who are the liveliest, healthiest, and enjoy their lives the most are the women who said all along, "I have my own life to live as well as being part of this marriage."

Enter any relationship with that attitude and your man will accept it and adjust to your lifestyle even if he's the controlling type. He will respect you more as well. If your man insists on being the only picture in the slide show of your life, he needs your help, and perhaps the help of others, to become more trusting and self-confident.

Of my own spirit let me be in sole
though feeble mastery.
—Sara Teasdale

~ 157 ~

I can replace a man's negativity
with positive thoughts and actions.
I will be positive for myself.

Josephine says: "The glass is always half empty with Stan. Say we drive by a restaurant at night. He'll take one look and say the place is closed. I insist we stop. Of course the restaurant will be open. The weird thing is, once he gets inside he'll have a great time. We would have missed a lot of fun evenings if I had been controlled by his cynical attitude."

Where you have dinner is a trivial topic compared to instances when a man is so negative he tells you that, in his opinion, you can't sing, can't write, or can't drive a car. He may be equally negative about himself or about friends. Anything can be the subject of a verbal attack by a critical person. Negative people are depressed. They want everyone else to feel as bad as they do. A negative man is also scared—of having his life improve, of having a good time.

Don't let a negative man's depressed outlook color yours. Remember that his negative point of view is nothing more than the opinion of a cynic. His words are not the truth and should never stop you from being yourself.

She'd been so programmed by Julian to think of herself as inferior material that if a man threw himself at her feet, her immediate reaction would be to call an ambulance.
—*Lucille Kallen*

158

Respecting each other's separateness in a relationship sounds good, but separateness makes me nervous. Achieving both separateness and closeness in a loving relationship will be a goal I will strive toward.

We've come a long way since a woman voted the way her husband told her to, yet although these days couples say they know that having separate lives and ideas is good, you may still be having trouble making that real with a man. There is a strong pull toward being together inseparably in a relationship, because different likes and dislikes can lead to anger—even though they shouldn't. Separateness can actually make for an exciting, vibrant couple.

Jill has had to work at achieving a separate life from Steve. They were both court stenographers and played on the city softball team, so they knew a lot of the same people when they moved in together. All was well until Jill went back to school to be a social worker. She now has a new world of friends. If she has to meet with study groups or work on projects with classmates, however, Steve gives her the silent treatment when she comes home. A few times when she's come home Steve has been out and never gave her any explanation of where he'd been. "You have your life, I have mine," he'll say. To improve the situation, Jill can try to reassure Steve that she won't leave him, even though some aspects of her life have changed. She can ask him to be supportive and not to act out because it will hurt them as a couple. She can make an effort to have special time with him so he knows she cares.

Partnership, not dependence, is the
real romance in marriage.
—Muriel Fox

159

I can survive without him. Demands,
sexual and otherwise, leave me cold.
I'm not alone in the world.

Ruth is a fun-loving, carefree outdoors-
woman. She's had a few boyfriends and
was married for a short time. She now
lives in the country, where she can go
horseback riding and ski. Ruth met
Louie at a ski race. They would laugh a
lot, ski together, and have a good time.
They often enjoyed going to a local bar-
and-grill after having spent a day outdoors. But on one occasion, Louie had
too many beers and got grabby and
bossy with Ruth. He ordered her to get
him something to eat, then he started
grabbing her in a sexual manner in front
of everyone. When she tried to get away
he held her arm in a lock. Ruth knew he
was drunk, but she was furious and
ready to kill him.

She left the bar without him and took a cab home. When Louie tried to get in later, she refused to open the door. Fortunately, he still had his own place. The next day she told him the deal—that he had to go to AA meetings because she believed he had a drinking problem and that he was never to speak to her or treat her that way again.

Louie told Ruth to go to hell and left. She stood firm. A month later he called. He said that he'd been to AA meetings and was grateful that Ruth had read him the riot act. A few months after that, they started dating again. Ruth got what she wanted because she had stayed firm and strong.

If sex is a war, I am a conscientious objector; I will not play.
—Marge Piercy

~ 160 ~

*I will examine my world with clear
eyes. Then I'll see that there are others
ready to be close to me besides a man.*

We wander through the day, coming into
contact with many people: colleagues,
store owners, friends, health club members, parents of your child's friend—and
we often don't realize that closeness is
near at hand. We usually don't try to
make an emotional connection unless a
crisis occurs. When couples split up, men
and women both tend to suddenly reach
out to those around them and find new
relationships to replace the closeness
they've lost. But why wait until he's history before adding more people to your
list of close friends?

Too often you have a wonderful chat
with the nice woman you've said hello to
for years just at the moment she is
leaving the office for a new job. Or you

finally talk to your neighbor as she is moving out. It can take little more effort than suggesting a movie or having lunch to turn an acquaintance into a friend and enlarge your world. A close support system is also the best insurance policy against the day a man decides to be with-holding. And he will have more regard for you with that caring group around you.

The one thing we can never
get enough of is love.
And the one thing we never give
enough of is love.
—Henry Miller

Index